Red Sky
at Night

Red Sky at Night

an anthology of
British socialist poetry

*Edited by Andy Croft
and Adrian Mitchell*

Five Leaves

www.fiveleaves.co.uk

*Festival Hall,
London, July
2003*

*to Haren

My great socialist friend
as Janfee, this was mine—
and, as a great gesture (
something very meaningful)
I am gifting it to Jan.
I know it will mean a lot
to Jan and Jan will love
reading
it! * X ☺
Ian*

Red Sky at Night
(ed) Andy Croft and Adrian Mitchell

Published in 2003 by
Five Leaves Publications,
PO Box 81, Nottingham NG5 4ER
www.fiveleaves.co.uk
info@fiveleaves.co.uk

Five Leaves gratefully acknowledge financial assistance
from East Midlands Arts

Cover illustration by Clifford Harper

Designed and typeset by
Four Sheets Design & Print Limited

Printed in Great Britain

ISND 0 907123 49 X

Contents

Preface
From a Building Site

The Left is a big country, a sort of Disunited States of Humanity. Many of its inhabitants wander from State to State, searching for Utopia or the Emerald City of Oz. But as William Blake, the greatest writer in this book, reminds us, the New Jerusalem is under our feet:

> The fields from Islington to Marybone,
> To Primrose Hill and Saint John's Wood,
> Were builded over with pillars of gold,
> And there Jerusalem's pillars stood...
>
> The Jew's-harp-house & the Green Man,
> The Ponds where Boys to bathe delight,
> The fields of Cows by Willan's farm,
> Shine in Jerusalem's pleasant sight...
>
> In my Exchanges every Land
> Shall walk, & mine in every land
> Mutual shall build Jerusalem
> Both heart in heart & hand in hand.'

Paxman: And just what is this New Jerusalem to be built out of, Mr Blake?

Blake: 'Pity and compassion — Lo!
The stones are pity, and the bricks, well wrought affections
Enamel'd with love & kindness, & the tiles engraven gold,
Labour of merciful hands: the beams & rafters are forgiveness —'

1

Paxman:	And I suppose this ideal community will come about in some rather remote century?
Blake:	Oh no, we're building it right now. Right here and now, all over the world.
Paxman:	I'm not sure I understand...
Blake:	Keep trying: 'I give you the end of a golden string: Only wind it into a ball, It will lead you in at heaven's Gate Built in Jerusalem's wall.'
Paxman:	Well, that's all we have time for tonight, now a quick look at the paupers...

I write as a mixed lefty, a socialist-anarchist-pacifist-Blakeist-revolutionary. But it's foolish to insist on only working with activists who wear the same logo. This book contains poems inspired by Mahatma Gandhi and Martin Luther King as well as by Marx and Lenin. Poetry has as many functions as the human hand. It can caress or tickle. It can clench and fight. It can work and create. Delight and struggle and creation and humour and song are all present in this book. It's moving and inspiring. It's a thundering good anthology.

As we've all seen, when socialists forget their humanity, they become a menace. Poetry reminds us of our humanity. Many of these verses will give courage to all of us who will never abandon hope for peace and justice.

The development of leftist poetry in Britain can be traced clearly in this book. And that poetry has made progress. In the first few decades of the twentieth century much socialist verse was fiery, but somewhat traditional, four-square and predictable. Some of those poems — with great exceptions like Wilfred Owen — could have been written in almost any century. But since the beginning of the Third World War in 1945, many of our best poets have learned to speak in their own modern language, using their own speech rhythms and slang and the beat of their favourite music. And so the incisive clarity of Alex Comfort, Christopher Logue, James Kirkup and David Craig is followed by the beautiful clearsightedness of Andrew Salkey, the beloved Jamaican poet, one of the Caribbean writers who opened the door for many younger black poets. In Alison Fell's 'Women in the Cold War' another door opens — the one through which so many fine women poets like Carol Ann Duffy and Jackie Kay made their wild and whirling entrances. Doors and windows opening — the visionary window through which Roy Fisher watched his strange survivors 'starting to make a tree', Edwin Morgan's window where he gazed and composed his great 'Glasgow Sonnets' and the hotel windows from which Tony Harrison wrote his socialist view of the USA in 'The Red Lights of Plenty'. These are mainly poets of my own generation, but I do think it has been a crucial period in socialist poetry. Of course there are younger voices singing now — Grace Nichols, Jean 'Binta' Breeze, David Grubb, Linda France and Mr Social Control — and there are plenty more to come.

So this collection gives me real hope, not just for the future of the poetry written by my brothers and sisters, but for the building of the New Jerusalem, which is going ahead, all over the world, stone by stone, brick by brick, window by window and door by door.

Read it forwards, then read it backwards, read it forwards again and then read Blake's poems. Nobody is more modern or revolutionary than William Blake.

Adrian Mitchell

3

Introduction

'By the end of the twentieth-century. Socialism had been rejected as an instrument of modernisation throughout most of the Third World. In what used to be called the Soviet Union it subsists, so far, only as a rallying call for those looking nostalgically to past certainties. In China and Vietnam, whose socialism had inspired the young in the 1960s and 1970s, capitalism, albeit of a special type, is being rapidly developed under the guidance of communist parties. Only in Western Europe does socialism appear to survive, battered by electoral defeats, uncertain of its future, suspicious of its own past.'
Donald Sassoon, One Hundred Years of Socialism

Socialist ideas and values, according to any definition, are in retreat across the world. Globalisation, modernisation and reform — banners beneath which the Left once marched — are now watchwords of international capital. Culture, which used to be an ideological battlefield between Left and Right, is now merely a site of private pleasure, public consumption and personal identity. Even right-wing social-democratic parties struggle to win elections. But if Socialism appears unfashionable, then how much more so does Socialist poetry. An anthology of largely twentieth-century British Socialist poetry suggests a kind of writing long past its sell-by date — worthy, naive, earnest, hectoring and, well, boring.

And yet no other ideology inspired and informed the lives and work of so many twentieth-century poets. A number of twentieth-century revolutionary leaders — including Mao Tse-Tung, Ho Chi Minh and Che Guevara — even wrote poetry. This was a major intellectual tradition, to which so many significant twentieth-century poets give their allegiance — Rafael Alberti, Louis Aragon, Bertolt Brecht, André Breton, Ernesto Cardenal, Martin Carter, Paul Eluard, Hans Magnus Enzensberger, Faiz,

4

Günter Grass, Zbigniew Herbert, Miguel Hernández, Nazm Hikmet, Miroslav Holub, Langston Hughes, Iqbal, Tom McGrath, Vladimir Mayakovsky, Pablo Neruda, Miklós Radnóti, Tadeusz Rozewicz, Carl Sandburg, Wole Soyinka, Tristan Tzara, Andrei Voznesensky, Yevgeny Yevtushenko...

Even in Britain, where cultural life is traditionally as wary of politics as politicians are suspicious of the imagination, poetry once enjoyed a natural — if marginal — place in the life of the Left. Poetry was a useful and enjoyable way for Socialists to articulate their concerns and to popularise their agenda. It also offered an egalitarian meeting place for professional and amateur writers, famous and unknown, Fitzrovian bohemians and self-educating working-class intellectuals. The very nature of poetry appeared to suggest some of the utopian values which Socialism tried to represent. Clement Atlee wrote poetry. So too did the Independent Labour Party MPs JS Clarke and James Welsh, and the Communist MP Willie Gallacher. In the 1930s, several British poets fought (and some died) defending the Spanish Republic against Fascism. In the 1950s and 1960s many poets were prominent in the life of the New Left, and gave their very public support to the Campaign for Nuclear Disarmament. The Scots poet Hugh MacDiarmid once stood in a General Election against the Conservative Prime Minister Sir Alec Douglas Holme. The Anglo-Australian poet Jack Lindsay once filled Trafalgar Square for a performance of his Mass Declamation poem 'On Guard for Spain'. The former poet laureate Cecil Day Lewis was a member of the Communist Party in his youth. Tom Paulin used to be a member of the Trotskyite Socialist Labour League. During the Miners' Strike of 1983-4, several well-known poets, including Edwin Morgan, Liz Lochhead and Linton Kwesi Johnson, gave poetry readings in support of the National Union of Miners. The ex-miner Mogg Williams once read his poetry to an audience of over a thousand people at the Trades Union Congress.

For much of the twentieth-century the relationship between poetry, Socialist politics and the Labour Movement seemed both common-sense and historically-justified. In his introduction to *The Penguin Book of Socialist Verse* (1970) Alan Bold argued that Socialism had a 'unique attraction' for poets everywhere, because 'Socialism has won the battle of linguistic usage, if nothing else. The word connotes progress, equality, protection from corruption, human mastery over initially hostile surroundings. Its various claims to have history on its side have won wide acceptance [leaving] capitalism... to determine its own inevitable atrophy.'

Unfortunately, Socialism has long since lost the battle for linguistic usage, along with much else. For most people the word is hardly synonymous with progress or equality, and not even the most committed of Socialists would claim to have history on their side just now. *The Penguin Book of Socialist Verse* is out of print as well as out of date. It is unlikely that Penguin are planning to publish a new edition. We believe that it is time to look back at the Socialist tradition in Britain in the twentieth-century and the poetry which it once generated. Of the 134 writers included by Alan Bold only 14 were British. Other valuable anthologies of radical poetry — notably, J. Bruce Glasier's *The Minstrelsy of Peace* (1918), John Mulgan's *Poems of Freedom* (1938), Jack Lindsay and Edgell Rickword (eds) *A Handbook of Freedom* (1939), Mary Ashraf's *Political Verse and Song* (1975), Clifford Harper, Dennis Gould and Jeff Cloves (eds) *Visions of Poesy* (1994) and Michael Rosen and David Widgery (eds) *The Chatto Book of Dissent* (1994) — have also sought to establish either its international context or its historical dimensions. This selection — for the first time — draws attention to the specifically British contribution to the Socialist poetic tradition over the last century.

For reasons of space there are many good poets whose work is not included here. This selection is meant to be representative and suggestive, rather than comprehensive, and it does not claim to be an authoritative record. We have included no songs, and we have limited our selection to poetry written in English. We have only included poets from the Irish Republic, the Commonwealth and elsewhere if they wrote their most significant work while living in Britain. We have made no attempt to define, still less impose, a version of Socialism on the book. There are many different kinds of Socialisms and Socialists, and there are many varieties represented here. No doubt some will disagree with our selection for political reasons. But we have not included any poem only because if its political sentiments. A poem has to work on the page, has to be a poem, before it can successfully carry any political weight or historical significance. A bad Socialist poem is still a bad poem. Because we have tried to avoid 'the enormous condescension of posterity', we have included poems which may seem now over-optimistic, credulous or even ill-judged; the story would be incomplete without them. On the other hand, for those who find the rise and fall of the Socialist idea in Britain in the twentieth century a depressing story, there are plenty of despairing poems in these pages. For better or worse, many British Socialists in the twentieth-century variously located their vision of the future in the organised Labour Movement, in 'Actually Existing Socialism' and in anti-colonial struggles in the Third World; these loyalties are unavoidably represented here. Moreover, the Left in Britain necessarily reproduced (and in some ways accentuated) the demographic unevenness of society. Gender politics did not, alas, enter the agenda of the British Left until the last decades of the twentieth-century. The poetry (and the lives) of women writers represented in the first half of the book are all the more important because they were, in every sense, exceptional.

This book, then, tells several overlapping stories. It tells the story of the movement of an idea from the eccentric margins of British life to the centre, and then out again to its disreputable edges. It tells the story of the — once commonplace — engagement by British poets with contemporary political events. It provides a sustained literary footnote to the history of the last century. And it tells the story of twentieth-century British poetry in cross-section — from the expansive rhetorical gestures of pre-1914 millenarianism, through the re-invigoration of national literary traditions in the 1930s and the popular verse forms of the war-time 'cultural upsurge' to Cold War empiricism and the subsequent long retreat into irony and despair.

Finally, we hope it demonstrates a kind of continuity between a rich and distinguished poetic history and younger, dissident, disparate and desperate voices. There is a new spirit of resistance and rebellion abroad, a new generation mobilised by the anti-globalisation and anti-war movements. It is not yet Socialist perhaps, but it contains the potential for a revival of the Left, in spirit, organisation and in imagination (the anti-war movement in particular has generated a good deal of notable poetry). The poems in the last section of the book courageously affirm that poetry is still a way of saying things that cannot be said in other ways ; a place of refusal and dissent, of public testimony and personal affirmation, of generous vision and imagination. There may be little or no space for Socialist ideas in the political sphere at the moment, but they are still stubbornly, vividly, present in British society and among contemporary British poets. If Socialist values are still in retreat, they have, for the time being at least, retreated into poetry. This may be good for the Socialist tradition; it is certainly good for poetry. And as the US poet Lawrence Ferlinghetti has put it, both are still:

'...the common carrier
for the transportation of the public
to higher places
than other wheels can carry it.
Poetry still falls from the skies
into our streets still open.

They haven't put up the barricades, yet,
the streets still alive with faces,
lovely men & women still waking there,
still lovely creatures everywhere,
in the eyes of all the secret of all
still buried there,
Whitman's wild children still sleeping there,
Awake and walk in the open air.'

Andy Croft

We Few
Against the World

From **The Four Zoas**

William Blake

What is the price of Experience? Do men buy it for a
    song,
Or Wisdom for a dance in the street? No! it is bought
    with the price
Of all that a man hath — his house, his wife, his
    children.
Wisdom is sold in the desolate market where none come
    to buy,
And in the wither'd field where the farmer ploughs for
    bread in vain.

It is an easy thing to triumph in the summer's sun,
And in the vintage, and to sing on the waggon loaded
    with corn:
It is an easy thing to talk of patience to the afflicted,
To speak the laws of prudence to the houseless wanderer,
To listen to the hungry raven's cry in wintry season,
When the red blood is fill'd with wine and with the
    marrow of lambs:

It is an easy thing to laugh at wrathful elements;
To hear the dog howl at the wintry door, the ox in the
    slaughterhouse moan;
To see a God on every wind and a blessing on even blast;
To hear sounds of Love in the thunderstorm that
    destroys our enemy's house;
To rejoice in the blight that covers his field, and the
    sickness that cuts off his children,
While our olive and vine sing and laugh round our door,
    and our children bring fruits and flowers.

Then the groan and the dolour are quite forgotten, and
    the slave grinding at the mill,
And the captive in chains, and the poor in the prison, and

the soldier in the field
When the shatter'd bone hath laid him groaning among
    the happier dead:

It is an easy thing to rejoice in the tents of prosperity —
Thus would I sing and thus rejoice; but it is not so
    with me.

London

William Blake

I wander thro' each charter'd street
Near where the charter'd Thames does flow,
And mark in every face I meet
Marks of weakness, marks of woe.

In every cry of every Man,
In every infant's cry of fear,
In every voice, in every ban,
The mind-forg'd manacles I hear.

How the Chimney-sweeper's cry
Every black'ning Church appals,
And the hapless Soldier's sigh
Runs in blood down Palace walls.

But most thro' midnight streets I hear
How the youthful Harlot's curse
Blasts the new born Infant's tear,
And blights with plagues the Marriage hearse.

The Fallen Elm

John Clare

Old elm that murmured in our chimney top
The sweetest anthem autumn ever made
& into mellow whispering calms would drop
When showers fell on thy many coloured shade
& when dark tempests mimic thunder made
While darkness came as it would strangle light
With the black tempest of a winter night
That rocked thee like a cradle to thy root
How did I love to hear the winds upbraid
Thy strength without — while all within was mute
It seasoned comfort to our hearts desire
We felt thy kind protection like a friend
& edged our chairs up closer to the fire
Enjoying comforts that was never penned
Old favourite tree thoust seen times changes lower
Though change till now did never injure thee
For time beheld thee as her sacred dower
& nature claimed thee her domestic tree
Storms came & shook thee many a weary hour
Yet stedfast to thy home thy roots hath been
Summers of thirst parched round thy homely bower
Till earth grew iron — still thy leaves was green
The children sought thee in thy summer shade
& made their play house rings of stick & stone
The mavis sang & felt himself alone
While in thy leaves his early nest was made
& I did feel his happiness mine own
Nought heeding that our friendship was betrayed
Friend not inanimate — though stocks & stones
There are & many formed of flesh & bones
Thou owned a language by which hearts are stirred
Deeper then by a feeling cloathed in words
& speakest now whats known of every tongue

Language of pity & the force of wrong
What cant assumes what hypocrites will dare
Speaks home to truth & shows it what they are
I see a picture which thy fate displays
& learn a lesson from thy destiny
Self interest saw thee stand in freedoms ways
So thy old shadow must a tyrant be
Thoust heard the knave abusing those in power
Bawl freedom loud & then opress the free
Thoust sheltered hypocrites in many a shower
That when in power would never shelter thee
Thoust heard the knave supply his canting powers
With wrongs illusions when he wanted friends
That bawled for shelter when he lived in showers
& when clouds vanished made thy shade amends
With axe at root he felled thee to the ground
& barked of freedom — O I hate the sound
Time hears its visions speak & age sublime
Had made thee a deciple unto time
— It grows the cant term of enslaving tools
To wrong another by the name of right
It grows the liscence of oerbearing fools
To cheat plain honesty by force of might
Thus came enclosure — ruin was its guide
But freedoms clapping hands enjoyed the sight
Though comforts cottage soon was thrust aside
& work house prisons raised upon the scite
Een natures dwellings far away from men
The common heath became the spoilers prey
The rabbit had not where to make his den
& labours only cow was drove away
No matter — wrong was right & right was wrong
& freedoms bawl was sanction to the song
— Such was thy ruin music making elm
The rights of freedom was to injure thine
As thou wert served so would they overwhelm
In freedoms name the little that is mine

& there are knaves that brawl for better laws
& cant of tyranny in stronger powers
Who glut their vile unsatiated maws
& freedoms birthright from the weak devours

Song to the Men of England

Percy Shelley

I

Men of England, wherefore plough
For the lords who lay ye low?
Wherefore weave with toil and care
The rich robes your tyrants wear?

II

Wherefore feed, and clothe, and save,
From the cradle to the grave,
Those ungrateful drones who would
Drain your sweat — nay, drink your blood?

III

Wherefore, Bees of England, forge
Many a weapon, chain, and scourge,
That these stingless drones may spoil
The forced produce of your toil?

IV

Have ye leisure, comfort, calm,
Shelter, food, love's gentle balm?
Or what is it ye buy so dear
With your pain and with your fear?

V

The seed ye sow, another reaps;
The wealth ye find, another keeps;
The robes ye weave, another wears;
The arms ye forge, another bears.

VI

Sow seed, — but let no tyrant reap;
Find wealth, — let no impostor heap;
Weave robes, — let not the idle wear;
Forge arms, — in your defence to bear.

VII

Shrink to your cellars, holes, and cells;
In halls ye deck another dwells.
Why shake the chains ye wrought? Ye see
The steel ye tempered glance on ye.

VIII

With plough and spade, and hoe and loom,
Trace your grave, and build your tomb,
And weave your winding-sheet, till fair
England be your sepulchre.

The Fine Old English Gentleman

New Version

(To be said or sung at all Conservative Dinners)

Charles Dickens

I'll sing you a new ballad, and I'll warrant it first-rate,
Of the days of that old gentleman who had that old estate;
When they spent the public money at a bountiful old rate
On ev'ry mistress, pimp and scamp, at ev'ry noble gate,

    In the fine old English Tory times;
    Soon may they come again!

The good old laws were garnished well with gibbets, whips
    and chains,
With fine old English penalties, and fine old English pains,
With rebel heads, and seas of blood once hot in rebel veins;
For all these things were requisite to guard the rich old
    gains

    Of the fine old English Tory times;
    Soon may they come again!

This brave old code, like Argus, had a hundred watchful
    eyes,
And ev'ry English peasant had his good old English spies,
To tempt his starving discontent with fine old English lies,
Then call the good old Yeomanry to stop his peevish cries

    In the fine old English Tory times;
    Soon may they come again!

The good old times for cutting throats that cried out in
    their need,
The good old times for hunting men who held their fathers'
    creed,
The good old times when William Pitt, as all good men
    agreed,

Came down direct from Paradise at more than railroad
    speed...
      Oh the fine old English Tory times;
      Soon may they come again!

In those rare days, the press was seldom known to snarl or
    bark,
But sweetly sang of men in pow'r, like any tuneful lark;
Grave judges, too, to all their evil deeds were in the dark;
And not a man in twenty score knew how to make his
    mark.
      Oh the fine old English Tory times;
      Soon may they come again!

Those were the days for taxes, and for war's infernal din;
For scarcity of bread, that fine old dowagers might win;
For shutting men of letters up, through iron bars to grin,
Because they didn't think the Prince was altogether thin,
      In the fine old English Tory times;
      Soon may they come again!

But tolerance, though slow in flight, is strong-wing'd in the
    main;
That night must come on these fine days, in course of time
    was plain;
The pure old spirit struggled, but its struggles were in vain;
A nation's grip was on it, and it died in choking pain,
      With the fine old English Tory days,
      All of the olden time.

The bright old day now dawns again; the cry runs through
    the land,
In England there shall be dear bread — in Ireland, sword
    and brand;
And poverty, and ignorance, shall swell the rich and grand,
So, rally round the rulers with the gentle iron hand,
      Of the fine old English Tory days;
      Hail to the coming time!

Song of the 'Lower Classes'

Ernest Jones

We plow and sow, we're so very very low,
    That we delve in the dirty clay;
Till we bless the plain with the golden grain,
    And the vale with the fragrant hay.
Our place we know, we're so very very low,
    'Tis down at the landlord's feet:
We're not too low the grain to grow,
    But too low the bread to eat.

Down, down we go, we're so very very low,
    To the hell of the deep-sunk mines;
But we gather the proudest gems that glow,
    When the crown of the despot shines;
And whene'er he lacks, upon our backs
    Fresh loads he deigns to lay;
We're far too low to vote the tax,
    But not too low to pay.

We're low, we're low — we're very very low —
    And yet from our fingers glide
The silken flow and the robes that glow
    Round the limbs of the sons of pride;
And what we get, and what we give,
    We know, and we know our share;
We're not too low the cloth to weave,
    But too low the cloth to wear.

We're low, we're low, we're very very low,
    And yet when the trumpets ring,
The thrust of a poor man's arm will go
    Through the heart of the proudest king.
We're low, we're low — mere rabble, we know
    We're only the rank and file;
We're not too low to kill the foe,
    But too low to share the spoil.

No Master, High or Low!

William Morris

Saith man to man, we've heard and known
That we no master need,
To live upon this earth, our own,
In fair and manly deed;
The grief of slaves, long passed away,
For us hath forged the chain,
Till now each worker's patient day,
Builds up the House of Pain.

And we, shall we crouch and quail,
Ashamed, afraid of strife;
And, lest our lives untimely fail,
Embrace the death in life?
Nay, cry aloud and have no fear;
We few against the world;
Awake, arise, the hope we bear
Against the curse is hurl'd.

It grows, it grows, are we the same,
The feeble band, the few?
Or what are these with eyes aflame,
And hands to deal and do?
This is the host that bears the word,
No Master, High or Low!
A lightning flame, a shearing sword,
A storm to overthrow.

Freedom

Ethel Carnie Holdsworth

Freedom comes slowly, but remember she
   Must beg from door to door, a barefoot maid;
No high-born dome in gilded car she rides.
   Full oft beneath the stars her bed is made,
And men repulse her often. Yet her eyes
   Rain drops of purest pity; as for hate,
It finds no entrance to her noble heart,
   And she will bless the toiler soon or late.

The thorns along the path of centuries
   Have deeply scarred her delicate brown feet;
Her gown is torn by many a thicket wild
   Which she has wandered through; her broad brow sweet
Is crowned by fadeless roses lovers placed
   To cheer her heart as on her way she came;
Her flesh oft faints beside the roadside hard.
   Her spirit cannot die — 'tis made of flame.

Comrades
in the Battle

For Whom

Jonathan Denwood

For whom and what is this foul slaughter done?
Tell us, ye rulers mighty in your seats —
And then shall people rising 'gainst their cheats
Drive you from senate, camp, and mart, and throne:
And not in continental lands alone
But here as well in England's snug retreats,
For even here most hellish work one meets
And yet scarce dare to make one's free thought known.

My countrymen, when Europe peace declares
Midst thousands of our noble soldiers slain,
Who but the ruling class shall reap the gain
In all the lands? Toil's slaves shall be the heirs
Of yet more arduous toil, and only they
Shall have to earn the tax war's debt to pay.

December, 1914

And It Shall Come

Albert Young

Strong men came from the Eastern way
  To storm the gates of the West,
In the heat and glare of a hateful day
  They came at hunger's behest,
      To end the wrong and to end the shame
      They came with eyes and hearts aflame
To burn the golden West.

Women sad, with hearts grown grey,
  And little children, too.
Came with men from the Eastern way
  To do what they could do.
      To gain the right of Life and Light
      For those who toil in the day and night,
And for little children too.

Oh for the end of the carrion class,
  And the crime of palace and slum;
Oh the fierce joy when the night shall pass,
  And the day of reckoning come
      When the morn sweeps down from the Eastern way,
      And the poor demand that the rich shall pay,
And the great be stricken dumb.

And as sure as time and the world go on
  And the sun sails the sky so blue,
The Earth will be cleaner and sweeter by far
  When it's clear and shut of you.

      So let it be: — and he and we are giving
      All that we have so the dead become the living,
      So we shall fight while the strength and passion last,
      And we shall win.

Dawn Behind Night

Isaac Rosenberg

Lips! bold, frenzied utterance, shape to the thoughts that
    are prompted by hate
Of the red streaming burden of wrong we have borne and
    still bear;
That wealth with its soul-crushing scourges placed into its
    hands by fate,
Hath made the cement of its towers, grim-girdled by our
    despair.

Should it die in the death that they make, in the silence
    that follows the sob;
in the voiceless depth of the waters that closes upon our
    grief;
Who shall know of the bleakness assigned us for the
    fruits that we reap and they rob? —
To pour out the strong wine of pity, outstretch the kind
    hand in relief.

In the golden glare of the morning, in the solemn serene
    of the night,
We look on each other's faces, and we turn to our prison
    bar;
In pitiless travail of toil and outside the precious light,
What wonder we know not our manhood in the curse of
    the things that are?

In the life or the death they dole us from the rags and the
    bones of their store,
In the blood they feed but to drink of, in the pity they
    feign in their pride,
Lies the glimpse of a heaven behind it, for the ship hath
    left the shore,
That will find us and free us and take us where its portals
    are opened wide.

To the Prussians of England

Ivor Gurney

When I remember plain heroic strength
And shining virtue shown by Ypres pools,
Then read the blither written by knaves for fools
In praise of English soldiers lying at length,
Who purely dream what England shall be made
Gloriously new, free of the old stains
By us, who pay the price that must be paid,
Will freeze all winter over Ypres plains.
Our silly dreams of peace you put aside
And brotherhood of man, for you will see
An armed mistress, braggart of the tide,
Her children slaves, under your mastery.
We'll have a word there too, and forge a knife,
Will cut the cancer threatens England's life.

The Combe

Edward Thomas

The Combe was ever dark, ancient and dark.
Its mouth is stopped with bramble, thorn, and briar;
And no one scrambles over the sliding chalk
By beech and yew and perishing juniper
Down the half precipices of its sides, with roots
And rabbit holes for steps. The sun of Winter,
The moon of Summer, and all the singing birds
Except the missel-thrush that loves juniper,
Are quite shut out. But far more ancient and dark
The Combe looks since they killed the badger there,
Dug him out and gave him to the hounds,
That most ancient Briton of English beasts.

May Day, 1917

W.N. Ewer

Spring should be with us — but spring is a laggart.
We are weary of waiting; and winter is long.
Slowly, ah, slowly, the boughs come to burgeoning;
Tardily, tardily, birds wake to song.

Over a year ago, flaming to westward,
Spring came to Eirinn: the dark Rosaleen,
Clad in white cloud, golden gorse and green meadow,
Rose in a glory of gold, white and green.

Now once again the old earth is a-tremble
With the joy and the passion and pulse of the spring:
Far to the eastward the new buds are blossoming:
Fruitful, O God, be the promise they bring.

Spring, that has come to the east — and the westward,
Soon may it come to rouse England again;
Come to her, red as her own English roses,
Red as the blood in the hearts of her men.

The Parable of the Old Men and the Young

Wilfred Owen

So Abram rose, and clave the wood, and went,
And took the fire with him, and a knife.
And as they sojourned both of them together,
Isaac the first-born spake and said, My Father,
Behold the preparations, fire and iron,
But where the lamb for this burnt-offering?
Then Abram bound the youth with belts and straps,
And builded parapets and trenches there,
And stretched forth the knife to slay his son.
When lo! an angel called him out of heaven,
Saying, Lay not thy hand upon the lad,
Neither do anything to him. Behold,
A ram, caught in a thicket by its horns;
Offer the Ram of Pride instead of him.
But the old man would not so, but slew his son, —
And half the seed of Europe, one by one.

Fight to a Finish

Siegfried Sassoon

The boys came back. Bands played and flags were flying,
    And Yellow-Pressmen thronged the sunlit street
To cheer the soldiers who'd refrained from dying,
    And hear the music of returning feet.
'Of all the thrills and ardours War has brought,
This moment is the finest.' (So they thought.)

Snapping their bayonets on to charge the mob,
    Grim Fusiliers broke ranks with glint of steel,
At last the boys had found a cushy job.

* * *

I heard the Yellow-Pressmen grunt and squeal;
And with my trusty bombers turned and went
To clear those Junkers out of Parliament.

Pity the Slain that Laid Away Their Lives

Iris Tree

Pity the slain that laid away their lives,
Pity the prisoners mangled with gyves,
Thin little children and widowed wives,
And the broken soldier who survives.

Pity the woman whose body was sold
For a little bread or a little gold,
And a little fire to keep out the cold,
So tired, and fearful of growing old.

Pity the people in the grey street
Before the dawn trooping with listless feet
Down to their work in the dust and the heat,
For a little bread and a little meat.

Pity the criminal sentenced to die,
Loving life so, with the world in his eye,
In his ears and his heart, with the passionate cry
Of love that will call when he may not reply.

Pity them all, the imperative faces
That peer through the dark where we sleep in our laces,
Where we skulk among cushions in opulent places,
With indolent postures and frivolous graces.

Eyes that prick the darkness, fingers thin
Tearing at hypocrisy, and sin
That batters the door and staggers in...
The streets surround with clamour and din,

Drowning our flutes, till the cries of the city
Flurry us, flutter us, force us to pity,
Force us to sigh and arrange a committee,
Tea-party charity danced to a ditty...

The scarlet ribbons flutter and wave,
A rebel flag on a rebel grave,
But to us the strong alone are brave
And only the rich are worthy to save!

Yet who shall blame us, plaited and curled,
Whose silk banners fly and the red flags are furled,
Flags that blow where the dead are hurled
Tattered and dripping with blood of the world!

Start a Revolution Somebody

Why I Choose Red

Hugh MacDiarmid

I fight in red for the same reasons
That Garibaldi chose the red shirt
— Because a few men in a field wearing red
Look like many men — if there are ten you will think
There are a hundred; if a hundred
You will believe them a thousand.
And the colour of red dances in the enemy's rifle sights
And his aim will be bad — But, best reason of all,
A man in a red shirt can neither hide nor retreat.

"Gentlemen"

W.N. Ewer

God placed the Russian peasant
Under the Great White Czar;
God put the Prussian worker
Beneath the Lord of War.
But He sent the English gentleman,
The perfect English gentleman,
God's own good English gentleman,
To make us what we are.

Our fathers once were freemen,
And as freemen wont to toil,
To reap the fruitful harvest,
And to gather golden spoil
But the greedy, grasping gentlemen,
The land-engrossing gentlemen,
The honest English gentlemen,
They stole away the soil.

They drove us from our villages
By force and fraud and stealth,
They drove us into factories,
They robbed us of our health.
But the cotton-spinning gentlemen,
The coal-mine, shipyard gentlemen,
Stockbroking, banking gentlemen,
They gathered wondrous wealth.

We toil to make them prosperous,
We fight to make them great;
But we know how they have robbed us,
We bide our time and wait:
While the fat, well-living gentlemen,
The easy, well-bred gentlemen,
The thoughtless, careless gentlemen,
Forget that slaves can hate.

42

The patient Russian peasant
Has turned and smashed his Czar;
Some day the Prussian worker
Will break his Lord of War.
And soon — ah! soon, our gentlemen,
Our proud, all-powerful gentlemen,
Our God-damned English gentlemen,
Shall find out what we are.

Shaking Hands with Murder

Osbert Sitwell

Native peoples
Can never govern themselves
In the way we can.
They do not understand
"Law-and-order,"
And will not develop
Their natural resources.
It is wrong to have
Natural resources,
And not to develop them;
It always ends
In the breakdown
Of Native government,

And then
The British have to step in
To restore "Law-and-Order."
We are a ruling race.
Wherever the British Flag flies
You will find
Law and order
— In India and Ireland,
And in Egypt.
We are determined
That Ireland
Shall decide her own form
Of government;
But we cannot give her
The right of separation,
Because we know
She would avail herself of it.
This would be wrong,
Because
We are a ruling race.

You have only to consider
Our Military and Naval Record
To realise this.

Look at Amritsar!
If the Huns or Bolsheviks
Had ruled India,
Law and order
Would have broken down,
And Natives
Would have been tried
— In cold blood —
And executed.
But we are different;
We are a ruling race,
We just send
For a General,
Who stops the whole thing,
Without any bother
About trials.
He simply brought up
Some soldiers,
And killed and wounded
Two thousand natives,
Who were standing about
In the street.
This will help you to understand
What is meant
By the White Man's burden,
And why
We are a ruling race.
Unorganised mobs,
Like the Bolsheviks,
Are incapable
Of ruling in this way.
They are merely
A brutal rabble,
Who will not develop

Their own resources —
Far less those of other people.
This is why
We say
We can never shake hands
With murder.
Not that I object
To killing, as such.
Wars, for instance,
Are unavoidable,
But I will never
Shake hands with murder,
Though I do not object
To shaking hands
With Suicide-whilst-of-unsound-mind.

The Indians are
A queer people.
They have no sense of humour,
And have been seen
To read *Punch*
Without smiling;
On the other hand,
They laugh
At things
Which do not appear funny
To us.

This is known
As insubordination,
And is why
Our General
Had to restore
"Law-and-Order"
At Amritsar;
For he knew
That if he failed
To shoot

Two thousand natives,
They would have laughed
At him.
To laugh at a General
Is, of course, very rude.
And I can never see
That it is funny
To be rude.
A good General
Can usually
Kill most of the people
Who laugh at him,
Either on his own side,
Or which is more difficult
On the other side.
The best General
Is the one
Who kills the most people;
Therefore, the best General
Is the one
At whom
The greatest number of people
Laugh.
(This rule, of course,
Applies equally
To the post
Of War-Minister,
And will help you
To understand
Why some Generals
And Military Dignitaries
Are so funny.)
But it makes it difficult

To serve under
A really funny General,
For if you don't laugh
When he means to be funny

You will probably be killed;
And if you laugh
When he doesn't mean to be funny
You will be shot
To a certainty.
This is one of the penalties
Of being
A ruling race.

The Image O' God

Joe Corrie

Crawlin' aboot like a snail in the mud,
  Covered wi' clammy blae,
ME, made after the image o' God —
  Jings! but it's laughable, tae.

Howkin' awa' 'neath a mountain o' stane,
  Gaspin' for want o' air,
The sweat makin' streams doon my bare back-bane
  And my knees a' hauckit and sair.

Strainin' and cursin' the hale shift through,
  Half-starved, half-blin', half-mad;
And the gaffer he says, 'Less dirt in that coal
  Or ye go up the pit, my lad!'

So I gi'e my life to the Nimmo squad
  For eicht and fower a day;
ME! made after the image o' God
  Jings! but it's laughable, tae.

As I Came Home from Labour

F.C. Boden

As I came home from labour,
  So stiff with sweat and pain,
I heard two starlings singing
  Above the long pit-lane.

Their songs were all of summer,
  And hope and love lives yet;
But I was sick and weary
  And stiff with pain and sweat.

They sing, thought I, of pleasure,
  And pain is never done;
They sing of ease and comfort,
  And comfort I have none.

There's naught for folk who labour
  But misery and rue;
No ease is theirs, no solace,
  No hope the whole world thro'.

And there I lingered grieving,
  And heard those happy songs,
And thought of all who labour
  And bear their bitter wrongs.

Luxury

Edgell Rickword

The long, sleek cars rasp softly on the kerb
and chattering women rise from cushioned nests,
flamingo-tall, whose coral legs disturb
the mirror-surface where creation rests.

Aconite, Opium, Mandragora, Girl!
Essential phials exquisite array!
Poisons whose frail, consumptive fervours whirl
the stony city to a fierce decay.

The churches' sun dried clay crumbles at last,
the Courts of Justice wither like a stink
and honourable statues melt as fast
as greasy garbage down a kitchen-sink.

Commercial palaces, hôtels de luxe
and Banks in white, immutable ravines,
life's skeleton unfleshed by cynic rooks,
remain to warn the traveller what it means.

The shady universe, once haunt of play,
in leafless winter bares its ways of stone;
the paths we shared, the mounds on which we lay
were ruled by Time and lifted by old bone.

Time has no pity for this world of graves
nor for its dead decked out in feathery shrouds.
The ghoul must perish with the flesh he craves
when stars' hoarse bells of doom toll in the clouds.

Children of Wealth

Elizabeth Daryush

Children of wealth in your warm nursery,
Set in the cushioned window-seat to watch
The volleying snow, guarded invisibly
By the clear double pane through which no touch
Untimely penetrates, you cannot tell
What winter means; its cruel truths to you
Are only sight and sound; your citadel
is safe from feeling, and from knowledge too.

Go down, go out to elemental wrong,
Waste your too round limbs, tan your skin too white;
The glass of comfort, ignorance, seems strong
To-day, and yet perhaps this very night
You'll wake to horror's wrecking fire — your home
Is wired within for this, in every room.

The Case for the Miners

Siegfried Sassoon

Something goes wrong with my synthetic brain
When I defend the Strikers and explain
My reasons for not blackguarding the Miners.
'What do you know?' exclaim my fellow-diners
(Peeling their plovers' eggs or lifting glasses
Of mellowed *Château Rentier* from the table),
'What do you know about the working classes?'

I strive to hold my own; but I'm unable
To state the case succinctly. Indistinctly
I mumble about World-Emancipation,
Standards of Living, Nationalization
Of Industry; until they get me tangled
In superficial details; goad me on
To unconvincing vagueness. When we've wrangled
From soup to savoury, my temper's gone.

'Why should a miner earn six pounds a week?
Leisure! They'd only spend it in a bar!
Standard of life! You'll never teach them Greek,
Or make them more contented than they are!'
That's how my port-flushed friends discuss the Strike.
And that's the reason why I shout and splutter.
And that's the reason why I'd almost like
To see them hawking matches in the gutter.

Ballad of the General Strike

Hugh MacDiarmid

I saw a rose come loupin' oot
Frae a camsteerie plant.
O wha'd ha'e thocht yon puir stock had
Sic an inhabitant?

For centuries it ran to waste,
Wi' pin-heid flooers at times.
O'ts hidden hert o' beauty they
Were but the merest skimes.

Yet while it ran to wud and thorns,
The feckless growth was seekin'
Some airt to cheenge its life until
A' in a rose was beekin'.

'Is there nae way in which my life
Can mair to flooerin' come,
And bring its waste on shank and jags
Doon to a minimum?

'It's hard to struggle as I maun
For scrunts o' blooms like mine,
While blossom covers ither plants
As by a knack divine.

'What hinders me unless I lack
Some needfu' discipline?
— I wis I'll bring my orra life
To beauty or I'm din!'

Sae ran the thocht that hid ahint
The thistle's ugsome guise,
'I'll brak' the habit o' my life
A worthier to devise.

'My nobler instincts sall nae mair
This contrair shape be gi' en.
I sall nae mair consent to live
A life no' fit to be seen.'

Sae ran the thocht that hid ahint
The thistle's ugsome guise,
Till a' at aince a rose loupt oot
I watched it wi' surprise.

A rose loupt oot and grew, until
It was ten times the size
O' ony rose the thistle afore
Hed heistit to the skies.

And still it grew till a' the buss
Was hidden in its flame.
I never saw sae braw a floo'er
As yon thrawn stock became.

And still it grew until it seemed
The haill braid earth had turned
A reid reid rose that in the lift
Like a ball o' fire burned.

The waefu' clay was fire aince mair,
As Earth had been resumed
Into God's mind, frae which sae lang
To grugous state 'twas doomed.

Syne the rose shrivelled suddenly
As a balloon is burst;
The thistle was a ghaistly stick,
As gin it had been curst.

Was it the ancient vicious sway
Imposed itsel' again,

Or nerve owre weak for new emprise
That made the effort vain,

A coward strain in that lorn growth
That wrocht the sorry trick?
— The thistle like a rocket soared
And cam' doon like the stick.

Like grieshuckle the roses glint,
The leafs like farles hing,
As roond a hopeless sacrifice
Earth draws its barren ring.

The dream o' beauty's dernin' yet
Ahint the ugsome shape.
— Vain dream that in a pinheid here
And there can e'er escape!

The vices that defeat the dream
Are in the plant itsel',
And till they're purged its virtues maun
In pain and misery dwell.

Let Deils rejoice to see the waste,
The fond hope brocht to nocht.
The thistle in their een is as
A favourite lust they've wrocht.

The orderin' o' the thistle means
Nae richtin' o't to them.
Its loss they ca' a law, its thorns
A fule's fit diadem.

And still the idiot nails itsel'
To its ain crucifix,
While here a rose and there a rose
Jaups oot abune the pricks.

Like connoisseurs the Deils gang roond
And praise its attitude,
Till on the Cross the silly Christ
To fidge fu' fain's begood!

Like connoisseurs the Deils gang roond
Wi' ready platitude.
It's no' sae dear as vinegar,
And every bit as good!

The bitter taste is on my tongue,
I chowl my chafts, and pray
'Let God forsake me noo and no'
Staund connoisseur-like tae!'...

The language that but sparely flooers
And maistly gangs to weed;
The thocht o' Christ and Calvary
Aye liddenin' in my heid;
And a' the dour provincial thocht
That merks the Scottish breed
— These are the thistle's characters,
To argie there's nae need.
Hoo weel my verse embodies
The thistle you can read!
— But will a Scotsman never
Frae this vile growth be freed?...

From **Gwalia Deserta**

Idris Davies

Do you remember 1926? That summer of soups and
    speeches,
The sunlight on the idle wheels and the deserted
    crossings,
And the laughter and the cursing in the moonlit streets?
Do you remember 1926? The slogans and the penny
    concerts,
The jazz-bands and the moorland picnics,
And the slanderous tongues of famous cities?
Do you remember 1926? The great dream and the swift
    disaster,
The fanatic and the traitor, and more than all,
The bravery of the simple, faithful folk?
'Ay, ay, we remember 1926,' said Dai and Shinkin,
As they stood on the kerb in Charing Cross Road,
'And we shall remember 1926 until our blood is dry.'

Rebel Tam

Joe Corrie

When Rebel Tam was in the pit
  He tholed the very pangs o' Hell
In fechtin' for the Richts o' Man,
  And ga'e nae thoucht unto himsel'.

'If I was just in Parliament,
  By God!' he vowed, 'They soon would hear
The trumpet-ca' o' Revolution
  Blastin' in their ear!'

Noo he is there, back-bencher Tam,
  And listens daily to the farce
O'Tweedledum and Tweedledee,
  And never rises off his arse.

From **The Angry Summer**

Idris Davies

What will you do with your shovel, Dai,
And your pick and your sledge and your spike,
And what will you do with your leisure, man,
Now that you're out on strike?

What will you do for your butter, Dai,
And your bread and your cheese and your fags,
And how will you pay for a dress for the wife,
And shall your children go in rags?

You have been, in your time, a hero, Dai,
And they wrote of your pluck in the press,
And now you have fallen on evil days,
And who will be there to bless?

And how will you stand with your honesty, Dai,
When the land is full of lies,
And how will your curb your anger, man,
When your natural patience dies?

O what will you dream on the mountains, Dai,
When you walk in the summer day,
And gaze on the derelict valleys below,
And the mountains farther away?

And how will the heart within you, Dai,
Respond to the distant sea,
And the dream that is born in the blaze of the sun,
And the vision of victory?

Fight! O My Young Men

D.H. Lawrence

Fight! don't you feel you're fading
into slow death?
Fight then, poor duffers degrading
your very breath.

Open your half-dead eyes
you half-alive young,
look round and realise the muck
from which you've sprung.

The money-muck, you simple flowers
of your forefathers' muck-heap;
and the money-muck-worms, the extant powers
that have got you in keep.

Old money-worms, young money-worms
money-worm professors
spinning a glamour round money, and clergymen
lifting a bank-book to bless us!

In the odour of lucrative sanctity
stand they — and god, how they stink!
Rise then, my young men, rise at them!
Or if you can't rise, just think —

Think of the world that you're stifling in,
think what a world it might be!
Think of the rubbish you're trifling in
with enfeebled vitality!

And then, if you amount to a hill o' beans
start in and bust it all;
money, hypocrisy, greed, machines
that have ground you so small.

O! Start a Revolution

D.H. Lawrence

O! start a revolution, somebody!
not to get the money
but to lose it all for ever.

O! start a revolution, somebody!
not to install the working classes
but to abolish the working classes for ever
and have a world of men.

The Mountains
of Tomorrow

Acres of Power

Randall Swingler

Acres of power within me lie,
Charted fields of wheat and rye
And behind them, charted too,
Brooding woods of beech and yew.
Beyond them stretch, uncharted yet,
Marsh and mountain, dark and wet,
Whence sometimes in my dream and ease
Strange birds appear among the trees.

The fields of corn are action's fruit,
Gripping the earth with puny root,
Their surface pattern neatly planned
Upon the chaos of my land.
Against the ruminating wood
They set a fence, but to no good;
The shadow and the sap of mind
Still weighs the harvest of my hand.

And the wild marches and the hills
Shut out by the imposing will
Yet hurl their livid storms across
To smash the fence and flood the fosse
And all his dictates and his laws
Cannot restrain that surging force,
For the whole land is my power still,
Divided, fenced, but no less real.

And one man only mourning goes
By day through the stiff planted rows
By night through the tangled wood, to gaze
On the vast savage wilderness.
The born surveyor, he that would
Turn the whole acreage to good,
Subject to one coherent plan
Dispensing the whole power of man.

But he between the fences dour,
This organizer of my power,
By rigid areas is confined
That sever impulse, hand and mind.
For he is only paid to see
That the fields grow obediently
And that the woods do not encroach
Nor the trees part to show the marsh.

For if the power that lavish there
Breaks into a sterile air,
Were planned and planted, fibre and juice,
And all my earth enlaced with use,
Then evil for his ruler's case
Whom to maintain in idleness
My fields of power are bought and sold
And all their goodness changed for gold.

Thus the land that is my life
Divided, ruled, and held in fief,
All the power it could produce
He cannot sell, but I could use.
And my surveyor, grim and harsh,
In secret now reclaims the marsh
That cultivated acres there
May bear a fruit for all to share.

Musée des Beaux Arts

W.H. Auden

About suffering they were never wrong,
The Old Masters: how well they understood
Its human position; how it takes place
While someone else is eating or opening a window or just
    walking dully along;
How, when the aged are reverently, passionately waiting
For the miraculous birth, there always must be
Children who did not specially want it to happen, skating
On a pond at the edge of the wood:

They never forgot
That even the dreadful martyrdom must run its course
Anyhow in a corner, some untidy spot
Where the dogs go on with their doggy life and the
    torturer's horse
Scratches its innocent behind on a tree.

In Brueghel's *Icarus*, for instance: how everything turns
    away
Quite leisurely from the disaster; the ploughman may
Have heard the splash, the forsaken cry,
But for him it was not an important failure; the sun
    shone
As it had to on the white legs disappearing into the green
Water; and the expensive delicate ship that must have
    seen
Something amazing, a boy falling out of the sky,
Had somewhere to get to and sailed calmly on.

Consider These, For We Have Condemned Them;

C. Day Lewis

Consider these, for we have condemned them;
Leaders to no sure land, guides their bearings lost
Or in league with robbers have reversed the signposts,
Disrespectful to ancestors, irresponsible to heirs.
Born barren, a freak growth, root in rubble,
Fruitlessly blossoming, whose foliage suffocates,
Their sap is sluggish, they reject the sun.

The man with his tongue in his cheek, the woman
With her heart in the wrong place, unhandsome,
    unwholesome;
Have exposed the new-born to worse than weather,
Exiled the honest and sacked the seer.
These drowned the farms to form a pleasure-lake,
In time of drought they drain the reservoir
Through private pipes for baths and sprinklers.

Getters not begetters; gainers not beginners;
Whiners, no winners; no triers, betrayers;
Who steer by no star, whose moon means nothing.
Daily denying, unable to dig.
At bay in villas from blood relations,
Counters of spoons and content with cushions
They pray for peace, they hand down disaster.

They that take the bribe shall perish by the bribe,
Dying of dry rot, ending in asylums,
A curse to children, a charge on the state.
But still their fears and frenzies infect us;
Drug nor isolation will cure this cancer:
It is now or never, the hour of the knife,
The break with the past, the major operation.

You that Love England

C. Day Lewis

You that love England, who have an ear for her music,
The slow movement of clouds in benediction,
Clear arias of light thrilling over her uplands,
Over the chords of summer sustained peacefully;
Ceaseless the leaves' counterpoint in a west wind lively,
Blossom and river rippling loveliest allegro,
And the storms of wood strings brass at year's finale:
Listen. Can you not hear the entrance of a new theme?

You who go out alone, on tandem or on pillion,
Down arterial roads riding in April,
Or sad beside lakes where hill-slopes are reflected
Making fires of leaves, your high hopes fallen:
Cyclists and hikers in company, day excursionists,
Refugees from cursed towns and devastated areas;
Know you seek a new world, a saviour to establish
Long-lost kinship and restore the blood's fulfilment.

You who like peace, good sorts, happy in a small way
Watching birds or playing cricket with schoolboys,
Who pay for drinks all round, whom disaster chose not;
Yet passing derelict mills and barns roof-rent
Where despair has burnt itself out – hearts at a standstill,
Who suffer loss, aware of lowered vitality;
We can tell you a secret, offer a tonic; only
Submit to the visiting angel, the strange new healer.

You above all who have come to the far end, victims
Of a run-down machine, who can bear it no longer;
Whether in easy chairs chafing at impotence
Or against hunger, bullies and spies preserving
The nerve for action, the spark of indignation —

Need fight in the dark no more, you know your enemies.
You shall be leaders when zero hour is signalled,
Wielders of power and welders of a new world.

The Butler and the Gentleman

Anna Wickham

The gentleman who had been at Winchester said
"When I made my first call,
After I took over that motor agency,
They showed me to the servants' hall."

He said how hugely he had been amused,
How a man's butler had been confused
To judge a gentleman, not by his speech, but by his face,
And show him to that ridiculous and most unworthy place.

While he told us this delicious tale,
I watched a woman delicate and pale,
With charming eyes and smooth gold hair,
Holding potatoes by the speaker's chair.
I liked the girl, and thought that he
Might choose to stay where she was doomed to be.

Hymn

Rex Warner

The splendid body is private, and calls for more.
No toy; not for a boy; but man to man, man to girl
runs blood, sweat oozes; each of us has a share.
All flesh is a flag and a secret code. Ring bells, then!
And throw away,
beginning from to-day
the eau-de-Cologne which disguised you, the stick which
    propped,
the tennis racquet, the blazer of the First Fifteen.
Don't kiss that dog, girl. Bachelor, your pipe is wood.
It is no good. Come away then. That must stop.
Some of you are still thinking what you might have been.
Don't do that, because it doesn't matter at all.

Come then, companions. This is the spring of blood,
heart's hey-day, movement of masses, beginning of good.

No more shall men take pride in paper and gold
in furs in cars in servants in spoons in knives.
But they shall love instead their friends and their wives,
owning their bodies at last, things which they have sold.
Come away then,
you fat man!
You don't want your watch-chain.
But don't interfere with us, because we know you too well.
If you do that you will lose your top hat
and be knocked on the head until you are dead.
Come with us, if you can, and, if not, go to hell
with your comfy chairs, your talk about the police,
your doll wife, your cowardly life, your newspaper, your
    interests in the East,
You, there, who are so patriotic, you liar, you beast!

Come, then, companions. This is the spring of blood,
heart's hey-day, movement of masses, beginning of good.

O poor young people! You, with the fidgeting hand,
who want to be understood, who want to understand,
now you must lie in the sun and walk erect and proud,
learn diving, learn to love, learn to hold a spade.
You who adore,
don't do it any more.
Give it right up,
and don't be a pup.
Isn't there anything on earth except your fidgeting hands?
Women won't help you, and it's a laugh to suppose they can;
and nor will stars; so if you can't get kissed,
don't bother to turn scientist and give yourself airs;
don't hide upstairs, but come out into the sun.

Come then, companions. This is the spring of blood,
heart's hey-day, movement of masses, beginning of good.

There is no need now to bribe and to take the bribe.
The king is flying, his regiments have melted like ice in
    spring.
Light has been let in. The fences are down. No broker is
    left alive.
There is no pretence about the singing in the streets and
    the dancing.

Come then, you who couldn't stick it,
lovers of cricket, underpaid journalists,
lovers of Nature, hikers, O touring cyclists,
now you must be men and women, and there is a chance.
Now you can join us, now all together sing All Power
not tomorrow but now in this hour, All Power
to lovers of life, to workers, to the hammer, the sickle,
    the blood.

Come then, companions. This is the spring of blood,
heart's hey-day, movement of masses, beginning of good.

Communist Poem, 1935

Valentine Ackland

'What must we do, in a country lost already,
Where already the mills stop, already the factories
Wither inside themselves, kernels smalling in shells,
('Fewer hands — fewer hands') and all the ploughed lands
Put down to grass, to bungalows, to graveyards already.

What's in a word? Comrade, while still our country
Seems solid around us, rotting — but still our country.
Comrade is rude, uncouth; bandied among youths
Idle and sick perhaps, wandering with other chaps,
Standing around in what is still our country.'

Answer them: Over the low hills and the pastures
Come no more cattle, over the land no more herdsmen;
Nothing against the sky now, no stains show
Of smoke. We're done. Only a few work on,
Against time now working to end your time.

Answer: Because the end is coming sooner
Than you allowed for, hail the end as salvation.
Watch how the plough wounds, hear the unlovely sounds
Of sirens wring the air; how everything
Labours again, cries out, and again breeds life.

Here is our life, say: Where the dismembered country
Lies, a dead foeman rises a living comrade.
Here where our day begins and your day dims
We part announce it. And then with lightened heart
Watch life swing round, complete the revolution.

To Some Young Communists from an
Older Socialist

Naomi Mitchison

Under the cold eyes, the car eyes of those young,
This car, cutting corners, into the ditch slithers;
And the middle-aged, mucky, stained and strained dither,
Feeling themselves fools, watched, their war-scarred
    withers wrung.

So we say, won't you help with the car, wise ones we
    want to trust,
But they won't — why should they? — they will walk
    fiercely, singing, with friends:
No drugs for the old duds, nor care for dud cars not
    worth mending,
Leave it and walk, they say, that's good enough for us.

We try to, walk, warily re-adjusting wrenched sinews,
But oh it's too hard, comrades, we can't, you've killed us,
    we're dead and done.
Leave us by road-sides, sunk, head in hands, it may be
    sunny,
Dreaming no more of the dances that fairies in fields
    renew.

As for the car, we don't care much, it had jolly gadgets,
If someone finds and mends and drives it, we mustn't
    mind,
Nor that, hoping to help, with you to give and take
    kindness,
We have been left to a fate worse than we once imagined.

Tolerance and irony were the things we once hated.
Now there is nothing but that — you've cornered,
  corralled the rest.
Look, our car's luggage of high violent hopes is only
  socks and vests:
Kick them away, careless, marching, you and your mates.

We who were young once in that war time, we are now
  not young but apart,
Living with photos of friends, dead at Ypres or Menin,
Remembering little of lies or truth perhaps defended;
We were hit then in the head, but now, hopeless, in the
  heart.

To Karl Marx

William Soutar

We who have won from the primeval wood
And are self-conscious of our heritage;
Keeping behind our breast, as in a cage,
These brute desires which still must be subdued,
Fear not the consummation of that feud
Prefigured, Marx, upon your passionate page
And rousing to fulfilment, in this age,
From the harsh jungle of our brotherhood.
Yet not the pity, nor the hungry lust
For retribution, nor the wrath made blind
By all the innocent blood sweated to dust,
Shall be the strength that fortifies our mind
For action; but the faith which scorns to mistrust
The magnanimity of humankind.

Second Hymn to Lenin

Hugh MacDiarmid

Ah, Lenin, you were richt. But I'm a poet
(And you c'ud mak allowances for that!)
Aimin' at mair than you aimed at
Tho' yours comes first, I know it.

An unexamined life is no' worth ha'in'.
Yet Burke was richt; owre muckle concern
Wi' Life's foundations is a sure
Sign o' decay; tho' Joyce in turn

Is richt, and the principal question
Aboot a work o' art is frae hoo deep
A life it springs — and syne hoo faur
Up frae't it has the poo'er to leap.

And hoo muckle it lifts up wi' it
Into the sunlicht like a saumon there,
Universal Spring! For Morand's richt —
It s'ud be like licht in the air —

Are my poems spoken in the factories and fields,
In the streets o' the toon?
Gin they're no, then I'm failin' to dae
What I ocht to ha' dune.

Gin I canna win through to the man in the street,
The wife by the hearth,
A' the cleverness on earth 'll no' mak' up
For the damnable dearth.

Haud on, haud on; what poet's dune that?
Is Shakespeare read,
Or Dante or Milton or Goethe or Burns?
— You heard what I said.

— A means o' world locomotion,
The maist perfected and aerial o' a'.
Lenin's name's gane owre the haill earth,
But the names o' the ithers? Ha!

What hidie-hole o' the vineyard d'they scart
Wi' minds like the look on a hen's face,
Morand, Joyce, Burke, and the rest
That e'er wrote: me noo in like case?

Great poets hardly onybody kens o'?
Geniuses like a man talkin' t'm sel'?
Nonsense! They're nocht o' the sort
Their character's easy to tell.

They're nocht but romantic rebels
Strikin' dilettante poses;
Trotsky — Christ, no' wi' a croon o' thorns
But a wreath o' paper roses.

A' that's great is free and expansive.
What ha' they expanded tae?
They've affected nocht but a fringe
O' mankind in ony way.

Barbarian saviour o' civilization
Hoo weel ye kent (we're owre dull witted)
Naething is dune save as we ha'e
Means to en's transparently fitted.

Poetry like politics maun cut
The cackle and pursue real ends,
Unerringly as Lenin, and to that
Its nature better tends.

Wi' Lenin's vision equal poet's gift
And what unparalleled force was there!
Nocht in a' literature wi' that
Begins to compare.

Nae simple rhymes for silly folk
But the haill art, as Lenin gied
Nae Marx-without tears to workin' men
But the fu' course insteed.

Organic constructional work,
Practicality, and work by degrees;
First things first; and poetry in turn
'll be built by these.

You saw it faur off when you thocht
O' mass-education yet.
Hoo lang till they rise to Pushkin?
And that's but a fit!

Oh, it's nonsense, nonsense, nonsense,
Nonsense at this time o' day
That breid-and-butter problems
S'ud be in ony man's way.

They s'ud be like the tails we tint
On leavin' the monkey stage;
A' maist folk fash aboot's alike
Primaeval to oor age.

We're grown ups that haena yet
Put bairnly things aside
— A' that's material and moral —
And oor new state descried.

Sport, love, and parentage,
Trade, politics, and law
S'ud be nae mair to us than braith
We hardly ken we draw.

81

Freein' oor poo'ers for greater things,
And fegs there's plenty o' them,
Tho' wha's still trammelt in alow
Canna be tenty o' them —

In the meantime Montéhus' sangs —
But as you were ready to tine
The Russian Revolution to the German
Gin that ser'd better syne,

Or foresaw that Russia maun lead
The workers' cause, and then
Pass the lead elsewhere, and aiblins
Fa' faur backward again,

Sae here, twixt poetry and politics,
There's nae doot in the en'.
Poetry includes that and s'ud be
The greatest poo'er amang men.

— It's the greatest, *in posse* at least,
That men ha'e discovered yet
Tho' nae doot they're unconscious still
O' ithers faur greater than it.

You confined yoursel' to your work
— A step at a time;
But, as the loon is in the man,
That'll be ta'en up i' the rhyme,

Ta'en up like a pool in the sands
Aince the tide rows in,
When life opens its hert and sings
Withoot scruple or sin.

Your knowledge in your ain sphere
Was exact and complete
But your sphere's elementary and sune by
As a poet maun see't.

For a poet maun see in a' thing,
Ev'n what looks trumpery or horrid,
A subject equal to ony
— A star for the forehead!

A poet has nae choice left
Betwixt Beaverbrook, say, and God.
Jimmy Thomas or you,
A cat, carnation, or clod.

He daurna turn awa' frae ocht
For a single act o' neglect
And straucht he may fa' frae grace
And be void o' effect.

Disinterestedness,
Oor profoundest word yet,
But how far yont even that
The sense o' ony thing's set!

The inward necessity yont
Ony laws o' cause
The intellect conceives
That a'thing has!

Freend, foe; past, present, future;
Success, failure; joy, fear;
Life, Death; and a'thing else,
For us, are equal here.

Male, female; quick or deid,
Let us fike nae mair;
The deep line o' cleavage
Disna lie there.

Black in the pit the miner is,
The shepherd reid on the hill,
And I'm wi' them baith until
The end of mankind, I wis.

Whatever their jobs a' men are ane
In life, and syne in daith
(Tho' it's sma' patience I can ha'e
Wi' life's ideas o' that by the way)
And he's nae poet but kens it, faith,
And ony job but the hardest's ta'en.

The sailor gangs owre the curve o' the sea,
The housewife's thrang in the wash-tub,
And whatna rhyme can I find but hub
And what else can poetry be?

The core o' a' activity,
Changin't in accordance wi'
Its inward necessity
And mede o' integrity.

Unremittin', relentless,
Organized to the last degree,
Ah Lenin, politics is bairns' play
To what this maun be!

Cokaigne Fantasy

A.L. Morton

The land
Of sun and sucking pigs
And lust made light
Is poor man's heaven.
Ah there the sweet white water
Turns wine on tongue,
Wind's tongue is tied
And man's
Tunes only to delight.
Light lie on glebe
Man's bones, and stones
Bear the back's burden softly
And a rounded image.

Man grows with time
In grace and gentleness,
Takes nature's mould
And nature his.
Subject and object fused
Race madly up to unimagined glory.
Cut cakes remain
And the roast goose delights with gesture's garnish.

So the old poet,
Mocked by philosophy six hundred years,
And by Jehovah's curse
On bread and brow.
And all the while
Plough turned and racketing loom
And toil grew tall
And all man's fate was darkness.

To the sound of the siren in the morning
Man goeth forth to his labours,
While the fountains of honey gush heavily,
Forgotten in Cokaigne's green dream,
In the idle delight that had grown
To seem foolishness in the earth's sight.
Till he awoke to Hammersmith and a fine morning
And a world washed white,
And the long night rolled over
And Cokaigne's delight not idleness
But toil new taught, turned and made light.

The Man Who Hated the Spring

Winifred Holtby

The man who hated the spring was cold and narrow,
   cold as water and narrow as a steel blade.
The wild white flowered dead-nettle, honey lipped,
The clinging goose grass, the gross and squatting dock,
   These were his enemies,
   He could not bear them.
Wrens in the hedge, the silent groping mole,
The fierce upthrusting spears of daffodil,
   Mocked him and outraged him; alone, aloof,
Adding his figures, measuring his plans,
   He moved, invulnerable and austere,
   Against the splendid chaos of the Spring.

So he planned roads and villas and a race track.
I will harness the Spring, he cried, I will crush it down
And his cranes towered to heaven, his drills devoured,
They tore great wounds from the hill, great holes in the
    plain.
With cement, with asphalt, with stone, with lime and
    with iron,
He bound and ground and subdued and crushed the Spring.

The starlings fled, and the moles no longer mated.
Away, away,
Flew the birds, the bees, and the unseen crawling things;
There was glass to glisten, there were poles to pierce the
    starlight,
There were light and music and engines and walls and
    men,
And the Spring? cried the man; the Spring is no longer
    here.

But he had roofed walls and bought walnut smiles and
    bath tubs,
Enamel, chromium, china, glass and tin.
There was a white door — to the Birth Control clinic,
And a blue door — to the ante-natal clinic,
And a bright green lawn alive with brown-limbed babies
In sunsuits of vivid scarlet and blue and gold.
Have you seen my Bobbie? My Lucy's cut her tooth.
The twins from Number Seven are doing well!
Darling, I love you! Little one, will you marry me?
At the Co-op dance in Unity Hall I await my love.
Where bindweed and daisy and nettle are driven to exile,
The lobelia glows blue between the crazy pavements;
Love, locked out with the moles and the mice and the
    badgers,
Comes home at night with the corporation tram,
And the Spring, the Spring, crushed by cement and iron,
Mocks from the laughter of girls, the bleat of the
    saxophone,
In the hurried rush to the shop for a new pink petticoat —
The Spring, the Spring breaks through.

Time and Tide, 7 March 1936

Hartmanswillerkopf

Naomi Mitchison

The barbed wire looks incredibly evil still.
Men were bleeding to death here twenty years ago:
Jolliment morts pour la patrie.
As I remember it, for years long life crowded under the wire,
Bleeding to death.
Doubtless the willow-herb came first.
Then came the saplings, alder, ash and willow,
Poisoned at first in shell holes, now more flourishing.
Next came the children, the boys, kind and embarrassed,
Interested certainly, as in the Moyennes Ages;
Dug-outs and arquebuses, trenches and boiling oil,
Machine gun emplacements, wire, bows and arrows:
Their war will be different

O Hero Akimbo on the Mountains of To-morrow

George Barker

Star crossed on its own limbs
I saw Spain like a rose spreadeagled to a knife:
The mountain muscles and the Gibraltar jaw,
The French forehead and the fist of grief
Seized by a sadist for a Caesar's leaf
Big on the head: browbeaten I saw
The face of Spain struck to a badge of war
For a king's coat, but to a heart's grief.

O hero akimbo on the mountains of to-morrow,
Star crossed spreadeagled and browbeaten Spain —
I see your starved shape grow more strong from pain,
Leap finer and freer from the grave of sorrow.
I see you go gallivanting on the hills again —
O hero akimbo on the mountains of to-morrow.

To Eat To-Day

Nancy Cunard

(In Barcelona, to-day's air raid came as we were sitting
down to lunch after reading Hitler's speech in
Nüremberg — *The Press*.)

They come without siren-song or any ushering
Over the usual street of man's middle day,
Come unbelievably, abstract, beyond human vision
Codicils, dashes along the great Maniac speech —
'Helmeted Nuremberg, nothing,' said the people of
    Barcelona,
The people of Spain — *'ya lo sabemos*, we have suffered all.'

You heroes of Nazi stamp, you sirs in the ether,
Sons of Romulus, Wotan — is the mark worth the bomb?
What was in it? salt and a half-pint of olive,
Nothing else but the woman, she treasured it terribly,
Oil, for the day folks would come, refugees from Levante,
Maybe with greens... one round meal... but you killed her,
Killed four children outside, with the house, and the
    pregnant cat.
Heil, hand of Rome, you passed — and that is all.

I wonder — do you eat before you do these things,
Is it a cocktail or is it a *pousse-cafe*?
Are you sitting at mess now, saying 'Visibility medium...
We got the port or near it with half-a-dozen,' I wonder —
Or highing it yet on the home-run to Mallorca,
Cold at 10,000 up, cursing a jammed release...
'Give it 'em, puta Madonna, here, over Arenys —
Per Bacco, it's nearly two — bloody sandwich it's made
    down there —
Aren't we going to eat to-day, *te-niente*? Te-niente?'
Driver in the clouds fuming, fumbling, unstrapping death.
You passed; hate traffics on; then the shadows fall.

On the simple earth
Five mouths less to feed to-night in Barcelona.
On the simple earth
Men tramping and raving on an edge of fear.
Another country arming, another and another behind it —
Europe's nerve strung like catapult, the cataclysm
    roaring and swelling...
But in Spain no Perhaps and To-morrow — in Spain it is,
    HERE.

September 13, 1938.
Written during the air raid.

To the Wife of a Non-interventionist Statesman (March 1938)

Edgell Rickword

Permit me, Madam, to invade,
briefly, your boudoir's pleasant shade.
Invade? No, that's entirely wrong!
I volunteered, and came along.
So please don't yell, or make a scene,
or ring for James to — intervene.
I'm here entirely for the good
of you and yours, it's understood.
No ballyhoo, what I've to say
may stand you in good stead one day.

I have to broach a matter that
less downright folk might boggle at,
but none need blush because we try
to analyse the marriage tie.

The voice that breathed o'er Eden laid
some precepts down to be obeyed:
to seek in marriage mutual trust
much more than sentiment or lust:
to base our passion on esteem
and build a home for love's young dream.
With this in mind, I'll state a case
Of interest to the human race.

Suppose a husband yarns in bed
of plans that fill his lofty head,
think what should be a wife's reaction
if he turned out the tool of faction,
who put across the crooked schemes
of statesmen sunk in backward dreams;
whose suave compliance sealed the fate
of thousands left to Franco's hate —

(those very Basques whose fathers drowned
to keep *our* food-ships safe and sound,
sweeping for mines in furious seas).
Our Fleet stood by, but ill at ease:
restive, our sailors watched the shore
whilst hundreds drowned who'd starved before,
victims of Franco's sham blockade —
though in the way of honest trade
Potato Jones and his brave lass
had proved this husband knave or ass.

Suppose he argues: Though I swerved
from honour's course, yet peace is served?

Euzkadi's mines supply the ore
to feed the Nazi dogs of war:
Guernika's thermite rain transpires
in doom on Oxford's dreaming spires:
in Hitler's frantic mental haze
already Hull and Cardiff blaze,
and Paul's grey dome rocks to the blast
of air-torpedoes screaming past.
From small beginnings mighty ends,
from calling rebel generals friends,
from being taught at public schools
to think the common people fools,
Spain bleeds, and England wildly gambles
to bribe the butcher in the shambles.

Traitor and fool's a combination
to lower wifely estimation
although there's not an Act in force
making it grounds for a divorce:
but canon law forbids at least
co-habitation with a beast.

The grim crescendo rises still
at the Black International's will.
Mad with the loss of Teruel
the bestial Duce looses hell;
on Barcelona slums he rains
German bombs from Fiat planes.
Five hundred dead at ten a second
is the world record so far reckoned;
a hundred children in one street,
their little hands and guts and feet,
like offal round a butcher's stall,
scattered where they were playing ball —
because our ruling clique's pretences
rob loyal Spain of its defences,
the chaser planes and ack-ack guns
from which the prudent Fascist runs.

So time reveals what people meant
who framed a Gentleman's Agreement,
and lest a final crime condones
fresh massacres with British loans,
should not its sponsor be outlawed
from power, position, bed and board?
Would not a thinking wife contemn
the sneaking hand that held the pen
and with a flourish signed the deed
whence all these hearts and bodies bleed?
Would not those fingers freeze the breast
where the young life should feed and rest?
Would not his breath reek of the tomb
and with cold horror seal her womb?
Could a true woman bear his brat?
No need to answer!
                           Thanks, my hat.

Full Moon at Tierz:
Before the Storming of Huesca

John Cornford

1

The past, a glacier, gripped the mountain wall,
And time was inches, dark was all.
But here it scales the end of the range;
The dialectic's point of change,
Crashes in light and minutes to its fall.

Time present is a cataract whose force
Breaks down the banks even at its source,
And history forming in our hands
Not plasticene but roaring sands,
Yet we must swing it to its final course.

The intersecting lines that cross both ways,
Time future, has no image in space,
Crooked as the road that we must tread.
Straight as our bullets fly ahead.
We are the future. The last fight let us face.

2

Where in the fields by Huesca the full moon
Throws shadows clear as daylight's, soon
The innocence of this quiet plain
Will fade in sweat and blood, in pain,
As our decisive hold is lost or won.

All round, the barren hills of Aragon
Announce our testing has begun.
Here what the Seventh Congress said,
If true, if false, is live or dead,
Speaks in the Oviedo mausers' tone.

Three years ago Dimitrov fought alone
And we stood taller when he won.
But now the Leipzig dragon's teeth
Sprout strong and handsome against death,
And here an army fights where there was one.

We studied well how to begin this fight.
Our Maurice Thorez held the light.
But now by Monte Aragon
We plunge into the dark alone,
Earth's newest planet wheeling through the night.

3

Though Communism was my waking time,
Always before the lights of home
Shone clear and steady and full in view —
Here, if you fall, there's help for you —
Now, with my party, I stand quite alone.

Then let my private battle with my nerves,
The fear of pain whose pain survives,
The love that tears me by the roots,
The loneliness that claws my guts,
Fuse in the welded front our fight preserves.

O be invincible as the strong sun,
Hard as the metal of my gun,
O let the mounting tempo of the train
Sweep where my footsteps slipped in vain,
October in the rhythm of its run.

4

Now the same night falls over Germany
And the impartial beauty of the stars
Lights from the unfeeling sky
Oranienburg and freedom's crooked scars.
We can do nothing to ease that pain:
But prove the agony was not in vain.

England is silent under the same moon,
From Clydeside to the gutted pits of Wales.
The innocent mask conceals that soon
Here too our freedom's swaying in the scales.
O understand before too late
Freedom was never held without a fight.

Freedom is an easily spoken word
But facts are stubborn things. Here, too, in Spain
Our fight's not won till the workers of all the world
Stand by our guard on Huesca's plain,
Swear that our dead fought not in vain,
Raise the red flag triumphantly
For Communism and for liberty.

David Guest

Martin Bell

Well O.K., he was wrong
Getting killed in Spain
Like that. Wal Hannington
Sat and tried to argue him out of going.
He was wrong, he was wrong,
The angel has not descended, the state
Hasn't the faintest chance of withering away,
And nobody is sure which way Hegel is up any more.
He was the greatest hero I've met because he was brave,
And would argue with anybody,
And could interest people because he was interested —
If he was so bloody interested he should have gone on
    talking, gone on talking,
Something might have been talked out.
Near to a saint, he should not have got himself killed,
Thereby making himself an ineffectual angel, a moth.
The Professor of economics was right:
He just couldn't keep still at a public meeting,
He would keep turning round and standing up to see
    what was happening and who was talking,
And this was probably how the bullet got him in the
    trenches at Jarama.

Poem

John Cornford

Heart of the heartless world,
Dear heart, the thought of you
Is the pain at my side,
The shadow that chills my view.

The wind rises in the evening,
Reminds that autumn is near.
I am afraid to lose you,
I am afraid of my fear.

On the last mile to Huesca,
The last fence for our pride,
Think so kindly, dear, that I
Sense you at my side.

And if bad luck should lay my strength
Into the shallow grave,
Remember all the good you can;
Don't forget my love.

For R.J.C. (Summer, 1936)

Margot Heinemann

No, not the sort of boy for whom one does
Find easily nicknames, Tommy and Bill,
Not a pleasant bass in the friendly buzz
Of voices we know well,
But not much changing where he goes
Divides talk coldly with the edge of will.

When he began, he talked too fast
To be heard well, and he knew too much.
He never had, though learned a little at last,
The sure, sincere and easy touch
On an audience and his handsome head
Charmed no acquiescence: he convinced and led.

Any movement, going north or south,
Can find a place for charm and open shirts,
The sun-bright hair, the lovely mouth,
But needs as much the force that hurts
And rules our sapphire dreams.
For seeing visions on the evening sky
I can do tolerably well; but I
Can read no blue prints and erect no schemes.

They fear the meddling intellect,
Cold, gritty, loveless, cynical, pedantic —
Rightly, had he no work but to dissect
Romance and prove it unromantic,
Breaking the scenery with his conscious hands.
But we are working towards a richer season,
And mean to plough our lands
With this unfruitful reason.

Thought, which our masters cannot use,
Walks on the slag heaps, wags on broken wires
At the old pit head, hears no news.
Thought rakes the fires
That keep our furnaces at even heat.
Capricious as a starving flame
Frail inspiration flickered till he came
To give the fire a world to eat.

A World
Set Free

What is Truth? Says Pilate

Louis MacNeice

What is truth? says Pilate,
Waits for no answer;
Double your stakes, says the clock
To the ageing dancer;
Double the guard, says Authority,
Treble the bars;
Holes in the sky, says the child
Scanning the stars.

Road 1940

Sylvia Townsend Warner

Why do I carry, she said,
This child that is no child of mine?
Through the heat of the day it did nothing but fidget and
    whine,
Now it snuffles under the dew and the cold star-shine,
And lies across my heart heavy as lead,
Heavy as the dead.

Why did I lift it, she said,
Out of its cradle in the wheel-tracks?
On the dusty road burdens have melted like wax,
Soldiers have thrown down their rifles, misers slipped
    their packs:
Yes, and the woman who left it there has sped
With a lighter tread.

Though I should save it, she said,
What have I saved for the world's use?
If it grow to hero it will die or let loose
Death, or to hireling, nature already is too profuse
Of such, who hope and are disinherited,
Plough, and are not fed.

But since I've carried it, she said,
So far I might as well carry it still.
If we ever should come to kindness someone will
Pity me perhaps as the mother of a child so ill,
Grant me even to lie down on a bed;
Give me at least bread.

Adam

Honor Arundel

On a dark night in a stinking slum
  In black Newcastle town,
A woman screamed in a big double bed,
  as her youngest son was born.

A son of England was born that night,
  For a life of glory and shame,
In hunger and dirt and a tattered shirt,
A laugh on his lips and a fire in his heart,
  And Adam was his name.

He ate and quarrelled and cried and fought,
  And learned to read and write,
And on shoeless feet in the grimy street
  Sold papers morning and night.

At fourteen he left the Council School
  With the three R's in his head.
A gentleman bought him a pair of boots
And sent him down to work in the pits,
He danced with the dawn up the silent streets
  To earn his daily bread.

His life was black from seven to seven,
  His mother took his pay
With a pint of beer on a Saturday night
A packet of fags and a cinema seat
  He passed his life away.

When they called him to go and fight
  He kissed his wife goodbye.
They gave him another pair of boots
And they sent him east in a steel grey boat
  To a sultry desert sky.

He stormed the machine gun nest alone
 In the shrapnel and the shot
The laughter had died upon his lips
 But the fire burned hot in his heart.

He stormed the machine gun nest alone
 While the bullets cracked around him.
With his red blood spilt on the desert sand
 The advancing soldiers found him.

They awarded him the Victoria Cross
 And the papers roared his praise
The medal they gave to his eldest son
In the stinking slum of Newcastle town
The shining medal arrived alone —
 For Adam stayed overseas.

* * *

Remember the barefooted newspaper boy,
 The boy who slaved in the pit,
What did he know of that fine word freedom,
 to light a fire in his heart?

Remember the lad who sweated and starved
 In black Newcastle town,
Must his wife live on in the stinking slum
 Must his kids know hunger's frown?

O brothers who handle a pick or a rifle
 In trench or shipyard or town
Remember Adam who fought for freedom
 And don't let Adam down.

The Farm Woman: 1942

Naomi Mitchison

Why the blue bruises high up on your thigh,
On your right breast and both knees?
Did you get them in the hay in a sweet smother of cries,
Did he tease you and at last please,
With all he had to show?
Oh no, oh no,
Said the farm woman:
But I bruise easy.

Why the scratched hand, was it too sharp a grip,
Buckle or badge or maybe nail,
From one coming quick from camp or ship,
Kissing as hard as hail
That pits deep the soft snow?
Oh no, oh no,
Said the farm woman:
But I bruise easy.

There was nothing, my sorrow, nothing that need be hidden,
But the heavy-dung fork slipped in my hand,
I fell against the half-filled cart at the midden;
We were going out to the land.
Nobody had to know.
And so, and so,
Said the farm woman:
For I bruise easy.

The tractor is ill to start, a great heaving and jerking,
The gear lever jars through palm and bone,
But I saw in a film the Russian women working
On the land they had made their own,
And so, and so,
Said the farm woman:
And I bruise easy.

Never tell the men, they will only laugh and say
What use would a woman be!
But I read the war news through, every day;
It means my honour to me,
Making the crops to grow.
And so, and so,
Said the farm woman:
But I bruise easy.

Shortest Day

A.L. Morton

Death the nimble, life the shy
Meet at the turning of the year.
Touching their fingers at the point
The sun turns in the southern sky
To start his climb towards the Plough.

Life takes a token payment,
Only in light,
For the frost's gloved hand bears heavier
And the wind's
Word of command
Stiffens the upright land
To strict attention.

Precious in this time
The minutes filched by life,
The hoard of light
Secretly amassed. For in them lie
The quiet bursting of the year's first flowers
And the unimaginable, singing summer joy, the hands
Of lovers and comrades linked and swinging,
The high-piled glory of a world won free.

Drawing You, Heavy with Sleep

Sylvia Townsend Warner

Drawing you, heavy with sleep to lie closer,
Staying your poppy head upon my shoulder,
It was as though I pulled the glide
Of a full river to my side.

Heavy with sleep and with sleep pliable
You rolled at a touch towards me. Your arm fell
Across me as a river throws
An arm of flood across meadows.

And as the careless water its mirroring sanction
Grants to him at the river's brim long stationed,
Long drowned in thought; that yet he lives
Since in that mirroring tide he moves,

Your body lying by mine to mine responded:
Your hair stirred on my mouth, my image was dandled
Deep in your sleep that flowed unstained
On from the image entertained.

The Voice of the Wheat

Jack Lindsay

I lay and listened to the long lisping sigh
of summer in the wheat. I drowsed beneath
the soft summer surge of whispering wheat ears:
it rustled with dry ripeness across the bird-lull,
a sea of summer surfed upon the stripes,
the lush tangle of hedge, the splashing clusters
of hawkweed splendid on the banks of sky.
For there I lay and over me summer flowed
in whispering waves, the rumour of the wheat,
till I could see the golden ripples swerving
across the sky, endlessly rustling, nodding
the thistle-blooms of purple.

Over all England flowed this sea of ripeness
between the bird-songs, deepening to sough
of summer, and I drowsed and drowned away
beneath it. Then two visions came to me.
I saw the past. I saw the future, too.
And both were knotted in my hands that gripped
the earth furrowed by the share of man.

I saw the peasants rise against the enclosures
again, again. With mattock and spade they attacked
the hedges of force walling the common-lands.
Throw down the mounds, the walls of private profit,
they cried and leaped and sang with blinding rapture.
Wild songs of islands blazing in the West
with fountains of red wine they sang, and marched
filling the ditches; and when night came down
a hood of quiet on the fevered brain
they lay and dreamed, and when the star-sparks crackled
the nightjar thudding in the valley heart
cried doom to the oppressors, the lovers moaned,
cradled in sweetness of hay. Those days went by

with dreams of valour for the tramping feet
and dawn swung up with a snarl of eager trumpets
crying doom on the oppressors, the yaffle yiked
its laughter, down on the water-meadow glided
the trilling redshank with his wings downpointed,
the apples loaded with coolness the russet shadows,
the deer sprang comely over the silver stream,
all, all for them.

I speak for those that rose
with Jack Kett or with Captain Pouch. A moment
they held the fate of England a single swathe
and lifted the sythe. They had the songs of promise,
the bullvoice of the noon, the heron-hour
of moonstruck musing, and their bubblepower
burst with the starwort glistening in the grass
and grappling with its delicate hooked leaves
to foamfade on the coasts of the year, gone
under the armies that the sheriffs led,
armoured and whistling with the wind. The peasants
died in the ditches they had sought to fill
or fed the ravens from the gallows elms.

It was a gallant march, but hopeless.
They had drunk wines of desperation trodden
from grapes that the moon ripened. They turned singing
back to the past. The past was a better land,
better at least than lives a grinding ass-round
under corrupted manorlords. They swarmed
singing. With hands or billhooks they attacked
the manifold barriers, the dividing lusts
of money, and they flung the hedges down.

But the invisible rifts and bars defeated them,
the enemy that they smelt but could not see,
could feel but could not grasp, the slimy devils,
the money devils, the vast net of credit,
the beelzebubs of usury. So they failed.

The men who with a reaping-hook stood up
against the whole world's might of greed entrenched,
the women who toiled breast deep in the waters
wrenching at dykes, the little children hacking
at the hedge-menaces sundering life from life,
they failed, all of them failed. The king's army
trampled them into the earth.

O peasants struggling for your common-lands
and losing England hundreds of years ago
O larkpulse of the morning, O throb of song
deep in the blue, are you not England still?
O longtailed titmouse nested in the thorn
I too have looked on England and loved England,
The story is not finished yet, O listen:
The sentry of the marsh, the redshank whistles,
the spring is here, and danger. Speak again.

Seeing the pattern of that defeated battle,
I saw within it, circling into birds,
another shape, another battle waving
its intricate banners. Like a cataract storm-wrack
over the leaping salmon-moon it hurried.
Battle within battle, I saw the future
mirrored in the past, though not the same
since men in changing earth with their desires
change their desires as well, and there I heard
the living voices which are freedom's voice
this day in all the shires. No Olton pools
broken by the solitary bird, no weirs
of silence in the sheen of willow-reaches,
no tarn of darkness cold with altar-stones,
but men and women saying: Unity
against the fascists.

I saw the time when the great plough of summers
guided by happy men will furrow across
the money barriers, the hedges of division,
I saw the great tractors of a people's power,
the combines of unity go crushing over
the walls of profit, the enclosure walls,
into the open fields, collective plenty.
And all that the old moonstruck peasants dreamed
now became act and knowledge fused and hammered
in one as steel-ore rivets to a bridge.
The cruel hedges splitting life with fear
went down, and over England the summer flowed,
the rustle of wheat, the surf of harvest-ripeness
gushed over England, there was no division
but summer's wholeness merged with human unity,
communal hands and electric power were one,
and the old cry of the hunted peasants triumphed,
England was commonland.

From **The Ballad of John Nameless**

Maurice Carpenter

One day I went to London
and strolled down Garrett Lane,
Where every year they chose a Mayor
For the fair land of Cockaigne.

Where Mr. Churchill's namesake
Wrote speeches for the folk
How one day England's people
Won't live like pigs in a poke.

And then I had a pint or two
In the "World Turned Upside Down"
As proud a Cockney as you'd find
Because I owned the town.

The people have one day in the year
When the world's turned outside in,
The poor are always with us, for
He lives inside our skin.

Oh Parliament's a private house
For landling and for squire,
Till our fresh wind goes blowing through
The stale and stagnant air.

So fill your glasses up and drink
To "Wilkes and Liberty"
Make Parliament the People's Voice,
Live Long, Democracy!

> We are the blood and the bones of our country,
> Common as earth, yet we fought for our say,
> Many who feel still live on inside us,
> Many who fall for the rights we enjoy.

Johnnie Frost, oh where are you off to mun
For some have got a pike and some have got a gun?
We march on Newport for the People's Charter.

I'll come along, for freedom is my right,
I am young, but not too young to fight,
Or march on Newport for the People's Charter.

How old are you, boy bach, George Shell?
Seventeen, and ready to march through hell,
Or march on Newport for the People's Charter.

"May the rose of England never blow,
The Clyde of Scotland never flow,
The harp of Ireland never play
Until the Charter wins the day."

Rise up, rise up, George Loveless,
Your spirit lives to-day,
Trades Unions in England
Defend a fair day's pay.

As once you stood up in the dock
Shouting "We shall be free,"
Against the blackest foe of all
We're standing up to-day.

The flame that burns in Stalingrad
In flesh and blood and bone
Belongs to you, George Loveless,
Not Soviet alone.

Man climbed the rungs of history,
And came into his own,
Belongs to you, John Nameless.
They shall not fight alone.

Oh where are you going young man in a hurry?
Take of your coat and get down on the job!
Our factory's already ahead of its quota,
But we'll not let up till we're over the top.

What is your name, young man in a hurry?
John Nameless I am and nameless I'll stay.
Unrecorded in pages I fought through the ages,
In freedom's last fight we are well on the way.

"Don't forget me," said the lass with a spanner,
I was a match girl and fought for my right,
John Nameless is leaving and I will replace him,
I'm turning the tools he'll be using to fight.

We reddened the water leaving the beaches,
"We shall come back," shook our fists at Dunkirk.
Hammered out history on Dieppe approaches,
Now at the benches our watchword is Work!

We reddened the water leaving the beaches,
Fought in the desert near El Alamain,
Now we're advancing our victory clinching,
Europe shall greet us and rise like a flame.

Millions are vivid this fight for a living,
Men in the past who were martyred and died,
Their struggle for freedom down centuries sounding
Rises superb as they fight by our side.

We are the blood and the bones of our country,
Nameless with Nelson sail out of the night,
Briton and Russian in brotherly action
Together storm heaven and let in the light!

So I, John Nameless, the English singer,
Saw pass me the pageant of a people proud,
So I who am English rose up from reverie,

Spat on my hands and applied me to the plough.
And Jack Miller to his mill to feed the folk,
Tom Miner in his mine, cutting the coal,
And John Nameless, too, stirring up struggle,
Working the while at weapons of war,
Men and masters in a common cause,
All manner of workers, both men and women,
Welding the weapons and shaping the ships,
Soldiers and sailors in solidarity with them,
And the winged men wheeling over Europe's horizon,
Welded together in daring of danger,
Lifting our spirits, awaiting the hour,
Waiting for a word, a call to the commons
To set sail together and break Hitler's power.

All Day It Has Rained

Alun Lewis

All day it has rained, and we on the edge of the moors
Have sprawled in our bell-tents, moody and dull as boors,
Groundsheets and blankets spread on the muddy ground
And from the first grey wakening we have found
No refuge from the skirmishing fine rain
And the wind that made the canvas heave and flap
And the taut wet guy-ropes ravel out and snap.
All day the rain has glided, wave and mist and dream,
Drenching the gorse and heather, a gossamer stream
Too light to move the acorns that suddenly
Snatched from their cups by the wild south-westerly
Pattered against the tent and our upturned dreaming faces.
And we stretched out, unbuttoning our braces,
Smoking a Woodbine, darning dirty socks,.
Reading the Sunday papers — I saw a fox
And mentioned it in the note I scribbled home; —
And we talked of girls, and dropping bombs on Rome,
And thought of the quiet dead and the loud celebrities
Exhorting us to slaughter, and the herded refugees;
— Yet thought softly, morosely of them, and as indifferently
As of ourselves or those whom we
For years have loved, and will again
Tomorrow maybe love; but now it is the rain
Possesses us entirely; the twilight and the rain.

And I can remember, nothing dearer or more to my heart
Than the children I watched in the woods on Saturday
Shaking down burning chestnuts for the schoolyard's
    merry play,
Or the shaggy patient dog who followed me
By Sheet and Steep and up the wooded scree
To the Shoulder O'Mutton where Edward Thomas
    brooded long
On death and beauty — till a bullet stopped his song.

Ballad of the D-Day Dodgers

Tune: *Lili Marlene* (Hamish Henderson variant)

Hamish Henderson

We're the D-Day Dodgers, out in Italy —
Always on the vino, always on the spree.
    8th Army scroungers and their tanks
    We live in Rome — among the Yanks.
We are the D-Day Dodgers, way out in Italy.

We landed at Salerno, a holiday with pay;
The Jerries brought the bands out to greet us on the way...
    Showed us the sights and gave us tea.
    We all sang songs — the beer was free,
to welcome the D-Day Dodgers to sunny Italy.

Naples and Cassino were taken in our stride,
We didn't go to fight there — we went there for the ride.
    Anzio and Sangro were just names,
    We only went to look for dames –
The artful D-Day Dodgers, way out in Italy.

On the way to Florence, we had a lovely time.
We ran a bus to Rimini right through the Gothic Line.
    Soon to Bologna we will go
    And after that we'll cross the Po.
We'll still be D-Day Dodging, way out in Italy.

Once we heard a rumour that we were going home,
Back to dear old Blighty — never more to roam.
    The someone said "In France you'll fight!"
    We said "no fear — we'll just sit tight!"
(The windy D-Day Dodgers to stay in Italy).

Dear Lady Astor, you think you know a lot,
Standing on a platform and talking tommy-rot.
　　You, England's sweetheart and its pride,
　　We think your mouth's too bleeding wide
That's from your D-Day Dodgers — in far off Italy.

Look around the mountains, in the mud and rain —
You'll find the scattered crosses (there's some which
　　have no name).
　　Heartbreak and toil and suffering gone,
　　The boys beneath them slumber on.
These are the D-Day Dodgers who'll stay in Italy.

For Edward Thomas Killed at Arras

Geoffrey Matthews

If you came dancing back
Lightly as draper, clerk, or tramp
Over the drab Channel, and walk now
The same ways as with Helen before the lamp
Dipped and the deer stole round you, sage and black,
Without our naming it you will know
The wind already carries a hint of lime
Along the ricks and cottages, and that
The fields are as warm today as a curled-up cat.
Today the sun shines gladly again for the first time.

You know this is the last
Spring, that leaves will dry their wings
And fly this year, and then appear no more:
Others will duck their heads in following springs
Under the raining hazels, or stroll past
Elm-hedges whose dark hair
Sparkles with buds like an old starling's back,
But when the seasonal boom turns for the worse
And the dead leaves are thrown down like lying
    newspapers.
We shall be downcast and come dancing back.

Draper and clerk and tramp, each
To his kindliest friends, the tiled town
With its machines, men, posters, turned again

Against the wrong enemy, the whorled brown
Rivers, or the Icknield Way, Even if I reach
Your ways and watch the green
Squeeze out between the trees' fingers to spend
another spring, we cannot ever talk
Or tell each other why the world must walk
Down this dark avenue, nameless, without end.

First Elegy
End of a Campaign

Hamish Henderson

There are many dead in the brutish desert,
     who lie uneasy
among the scrub in this landscape of half-wit
stunted ill-will. For the dead land is insatiate
and necrophilous. The sand is blowing about still.
Many who for various reasons, or because
     of mere unanswerable compulsion, came here
and fought among the clutching gravestones,
     shivered and sweated,
cried out, suffered thirst, were stoically silent, cursed
the spittering machine-guns, were homesick for Europe
and fast embedded in quicksand of Africa
     agonized and died.
And sleep now. Sleep here the sleep of the dust.

There were our own, there were the others.
Their deaths were like their lives, human and animal.
There were no gods and precious few heroes.
What they regretted when they died had nothing to do
     with race and leader, realm indivisible,
laboured Augustan speeches or vague imperial heritage.
(They saw through that guff before the axe fell.)
     Their longing turned to
the lost world glimpsed in the memory of letters:
an evening at the pictures in the friendly dark,

two knowing conspirators smiling and whispering secrets;
  or else
a family gathering in the homely kitchen
with Mum so proud of her boys in uniform:
  their thoughts trembled
between moments of estrangement, and ecstatic moments
of reconciliation: and their desire
crucified itself against the unutterable shadow of someone
whose photo was in their wallets.
Then death made his incision.

There were our own, there were the others.
Therefore, minding the great word of Glencoe's
son, that we should not disfigure ourselves
with villainy of hatred; and seeing that all
have gone down like curs into anonymous silence,
I will bear witness for I knew the others.
Seeing that littoral and interior are alike indifferent
and the birds are drawn again to our welcoming north
why should I not sing *them*, the dead, the innocent?

Drinking Song

Randall Swingler

The pub is the place where good comrades are found,
For the day's work is done so we'll call one more round.
Be it cider or guinness or fine tawny port
Or gin by the gill or good ale by the quart.

Here's a plague on the brewer who waters it down,
Till you can't tell the difference 'tween bitter and brown,
And another on the Government that taxes our beer
While profits are mounting by millions a year.

Damnation to the martyr, the saint and the prig,
Whose bladders are too small and whose pride is too big.
And the worst we can wish them is the hell that they fear
A tropical country where you can't buy a beer.

Here's a health to the Red Army whom Hitler detests
And the kick in the panzers we'll give in the west,
Here's a health to the Soviets where the lads own the land
And here's to the day when all workers join hands.

Here's a health to our freedom and may it grow great:
When we take a hand in controlling the state
We'll clear out the fakers and the fat profiteers
And throw all the big-wigs outside on their ears.

Then all may be happy and work with a will,
For we'll own the factory, the farm and the mill,
And when ale's brewed for drinking and not for profit's sake
We'll put plenty of hops in and avoid belly-ache.

So lift up your elbows and lift 'em up high
And tip up your glasses till the heel taps the sky
We'll drink to each other and drink to the day
When working men and women have it all their own way.

Stalingrad: 1942

Norman Nicholson

The broken sandstone slabs litter the shore
Like gingerbread; the shingle, pink and grey,
Slants to the runnels of the rocky floor
Where seaweed greens the red edge of the sea.

The tide rides up from Ireland, and a peel
Of sun curls round the axles of the waves;
The rough tongue of the water like the steel
Tongue of a limpet strops the kerb of caves.

Stalingrad now has stood the flood of fire,
Three moons of tide, for more than eighty days;
And this for more than eighty hundred year
Has borne the barrage of the western seas.

Whatever names wash over Stalingrad,
Or salt corrodes its stone, or torrents shock
Its cliffs, the city will not change, though blood
Settle like ore in the red veins of rock.

Ballad of the Taxi Driver's Cap

(Tune: *The Lincolnshire Poacher:* to a refrain by Maurice James Craig)

Hamish Henderson

O Hitler's a non-smoker
and Churchill smokes cigars
and they're both as keen as mustard
on imperialistic wars.
But your uncle Joe's a worker
and a very decent chap
because he smokes a pipe and wears
a taxi-driver's cap.

When Rommel got to Alamein
and shook the British line
the whole of Cairo beat it to
the land of Palestine.
But Moscow's never raised a yell
and never had a flap
because Joe smokes a pipe and wears
a taxi-driver's cap.

That Hitler's armies can't be beat
is just a lot of cock,
for Marshal Timoshenko's boys
are pissing through von Bock.
The Fuehrer makes the bloomers
and his Marshals take the rap;
Meanwhile Joe smokes a pipe and wears
a taxi-driver's cap.

The Fascist drive on Stalingrad
is going mighty slow.
They've got a room in Number Nine
of Slobberskaya Row.
When Fascist armies start to run
old Gobbels fills the gap.
Meanwhile Joe smokes a pipe and wears
a taxi-driver's cap!

At home those beggars publicise
the deeds of "our Ally"
whose dearest wish was once to biff
the Bolshie in the eye.
Your uncle Joe is wise to this;
he isn't such a sap
although he smokes a pipe and wears
a taxi-driver's cap!

Comrade Laughter

Paul Potts

Get yourself elected
On to their committees
Put hunger on the dole
And misery
Up against a wall
Forever.

Good morning, Comrade Laughter,
There's plenty of work
For you here.

The Day the War Ended...

Randall Swingler

On the day the war ended
The sun laced the avenues with lime-tree scent
The silver birches danced on the sidewalk
And the girls came out like tulips in their colours:

Only the soldiers were caught, like sleepwalkers
Wakened unaware, naked there in the street.
Fatuous in flowers, their tanks, tamed elephants,
Wallowed among the crowds in the square.

There is a moment when contradictions cross,
A split of a moment when history twirls on one toe
Like a ballerina, and all men are really equal
And happiness could be impartial for once —

Only the soldier, snatched by the sudden stop
In his world's turning, whirled like a meteor
Through a phoenix night of stars, is falling, falling

And as his trajectory bows and earth begins
To pull again, his hollow ears are moaning
With a wild tone of sorrow and the loss, the loss...

Gradisca: May, 1945.

Cold Wind

Victory Bonfire

Ruth Pitter

It is a legend already: a wide wide stubble,
Barley-stubble, a hundred pale acres,
With a mountain of straw stacked in the middle,
    towering, looming,
Big as a small hotel. They had ploughed round it
Thirty furrows for a firebreak,
Right away from the house, outbuildings, stackyard,
Right away from the coppice, orchard, hedges:
And high-climbing boys had planted an image of Hitler
On the lonely summit, Adolf forlornly leering.

We made ourselves nests of straw on the edge of the
    stubble,
In a sweet September twilight, a full moon rising
Far out on the blond landscape, as if at sea,
And the mighty berg of straw was massive before us;
Barley-straw, full of weed-seeds, fit only for burning;
House and barn and low buildings little and hull-down
    yonder.
People were wandering in, the children noisy, a rumour
    of fireworks
Rife among them; the infants never had seen any.
We sat attentive. In their straw nests, the smallest
Piled themselves lovingly on each other.
Now the farmer's four young ones
Stalked over the ploughed strip, solemn with purpose.

Wisps of smoke at the four corners —
Tongues of flame on the still blue evening,
And she's away!... A pause, a crackle, a roar!
Sheets of orange flame in a matter of seconds —
And in a matter of minutes — hypnotised minutes —
Vast caverns of embers, volcanoes gushing and blushing,
Whizening wafts on cliffs and valleys of hell,

Quivering cardinal-coloured glens and highlands,
Great masses panting, pulsating, lunglike and scarlet,
Fireballs, globes of pure incandescence
Soaring up like balloons, formal and dreadful,
Threatening the very heavens. The moon climbing
Shakes like a jelly through heated air — it's Hitler!
Look. Look! Hitler's ghost! Cheering and screaming —
Some not quite sure how they like it. Now Daddy Foster
Springs a surprise — he's touched off some rockets.
    O murder!
Knife-edged shrieks from half the young entry!
Buzz-saw howls from the wartime vintage,
For a rocket can only be a V2,
A firecracker a thermite bomb. O hang Daddy Foster!
(So mighty in energy, mighty in influence,
Able to get unobtainable fireworks through Business
    Contacts.)
There are mothers retreating, taking their weepers with
    them.
With jangled nerves they execrate Daddy Foster.
Giving him little glory of Business Contacts,
And wondering how long it will be before their infants
Are quiet in their beds. And fireworks will be a lot
    cheaper
Before they or theirs will squander a sixpence on them
Little girls from the farm bring lapfuls of apples
From the orchard yonder, picked in the moonlight.
They know the kinds by the shape of the trunks,
So often they've climbed there. These are the earlies,
Worcester Pearmain and Miller's Seedling,
Hard and red in one skirt, soft, milky-pale in the other.
There are drinks, sandwiches, ice-cream out of the
    baskets,
The glow of the gleed on our faces. and elsewhere
Autumn chill creeping. Into the straw we burrow,
Murmuring and calling, getting colder and sleepier,
And the awns of the barley are working into our souls —
(*Troppo mustachio*, says the Eyetye prisoner)

And the fire is falling and high and haughty the moon
Shows us our homeward path. Good-nights, then silence:
And the mole-cricket clinks alone, and the stubbies are
    vacant,
Only blushing and whitening embers left fading and
    falling.

August 6, 1945

Alison Fell

In the Enola Gay
five minutes before impact
he whistles a dry tune

Later he will say
that the whole blooming sky
went up like an apricot ice.
Later he will laugh and tremble
at such a surrender, for the eye
of his belly saw Marilyn's skirts
fly over her head for ever

On the river bank,
bees drizzle over
hot white rhododendrons

Later she will walk
the dust, a scarlet girl
with her whole stripped skin
at her heel, stuck like an old
shoe sole or mermaid's tail

Later she will lie down
in the flecked black ash
where the people are become
as lizards or salamanders
and, blinded, she will complain:
Mother you are late, so late

Later in dreams he will look
down shrieking and see
          ladybirds
          ladybirds

From **My Song is for All Men**

Peter Blackman

Sometimes all night I kept vigil with men stripped of
their flesh
by pitiless hunger in the prison camps of the Nazis
I had heard this hunger sobbing before in the wide weary
eyes of children
In Oldham West Indies Africa London wreathing dead
skins round high harvest
In Ireland India China
That those who despise our humanity should add ten
more per cent to their dividends
These things happened then not behind the curtain of
war
But in the times they name peace in the streets on the
farms
Among the sharecroppers white and black in Virginia
Glad to fill their bellies with earth when the factor had
stolen their maize and their cotton
Among the poor whites and the Zulus coloureds and
Hottentots who live at the Cape
Among the sun-browned fields of Missouri where they
ploughed back the corn
Because those who planted it had no money to buy it
In Grimsby where they gave the night's catch back to the
sea
For men may not eat fish when they have no money to
buy it
In Brazil where they fed the coffee as fuel to engines
In Argentine as they slaughtered the cattle since millions
in China
Shall not eat flesh because they have no money to buy it
In Belsen Auschwitz Buchenwald the murder was
somewhat more ordered
Vastness was all, gas but the sign of a superior
civilisation

Oh men of Europe Africa Asia America Australia and all
    the sea islands
These men feed on our flesh like a cancer
War is but the end of their logic
Let us then dress the bill of our claims let us examine
    them
Comrades and friends it is to you I am speaking not to
    the others

I know all your sorrow brothers the years have revealed it
My flesh winced as the rough horse-hide stripped Zoya
    naked
The rude sjambok tearing a Zulu in Orange Free State
Still wakes my sleep in a nightmare,
On my heart is a rose a red rose a whole land scarleted
    courage
For the roses are red in Korea all the earth is a rose
    staunched in the blood of its people
Red as the star that shall sit in the triumph this people
    will win

Let us then dress the bill of our claims let us dress them
    confidently
For the shouts of the battle rise a roar of wild waters
Crying triumph at Stalingrad
A fury of anger floods madly through China sweeping
    corruption swift to the sea
All around me thunder the peasants loud-throated
    greeting the soldiers
They have come a long march all the days of the year
    over high mountains
To bring us this peace
Their feet are bright on the hillside bivouacking the
    morning
From Paris Morocco AIaska Calcutta the echoes come
    back to batter the door of my prison

Brown hands black hands white hands yellow hands
Flatten the walls of my cell
Now I go into the daylight to continue my song, my song
    this strong hope
The pledge that today we shall live the assurance of all
    our tomorrows
Here the one chant we may raise at this time
For the men of our class for their joy in their living
Their courage wherever we find them

And you Julius, Zoya, Danielle, Peri
You with the thousands known to us the thousands
    whose names are denied us
I greet as I go forth to the morning free because you kept
    faith
I go like you to keep faith with the living

Over the years strong voices rise
from the springtime of our living

And I the black poet I answer these voices
For these voices are mine
I may not forget these though oceans divide us
For their sorrow is child of my sorrow my pain is their
    pain
My joy theirs to rejoice in, their song my remembrancer
I sing as I bind the stoops in the cane fields of Cuba
Where I hew out the gold at the Cape or the coal in
    Virginia
See the morning is bright our strength opens the gate of
    tomorrow

Let me then name them let me remember them here let
    me praise them
Those who have lent light to my living
Rising a chorus comes with them Jan Drda spent like a
    fountain of merriment
Emi Siao lending soft kindness to all who come near him

143

Pablo Neruda vast as the Andes bordering every horizon
They come with their peoples of Asia Europe and all the
    Americas

With them also I remember with praise
All who alike individually and in thought banded
    together share my hope in the human
I remember the Christian if in peace he will walk as my
    travelling companion
I remember the Muslim strong at my side as a brother
I welcome the learned and all who can spell me ways and
    methods of doing
I remember John Brown for his courage and manhood
    still march on in America
Highest above all let me praise Marx Lenin and Stalin
Marx for he taught us our power the strength we
    enfolded together
Stripped bare the false mysteries our enemies clogged in
    our seeing
Lenin who made this truth clean clear as a fountain our
    common possession
Lenin man's best of men touching bright as a summer sun
The heart unspoilt by hate of its fellows
Stalin who labours that in each this truth shall root in its
    glory

In these and with these I remember the ordinary man in
    any street or village
Who ever held out to me the hand of a brother
I grasp this hand wherever I find it in Perth Paris
    Prague New York Buenos Aires Pekin
This hand piled flowers in my praise red roses in Prague
All the earth's blooms gathered in Moscow
I hold with particular tenderness the hand of a German
    woman
Fled from the Nazis because she saw herself demeaned in
    their thinking about me
Look this is a white hand it is my hand I am the black man.

I hear strong voices calling me brother from the rough
   horse-hair tents of Mongolia
In Korea the rivers and mountains leap with the cry of
   their welcome
My heart sings in the lilt of the tear-twisted caress from
   the mountains and far lands of China
I gather like greeting from the red roughened hands of
   the steelmen of Sheffield
My smile is the smile of the miner descending the
   coalpits of Rhondda
I am by the side of the stevedore heaving bales in the
   shipyards of Antwerp
I reach around earth to embrace the Australian docker
For his handclasp assures me victory over subtly plotted
   deception
These are my strength my force their varied conceivings
My calm that in them my living may never decay

And since I am of Africa all that is Africa comes with me
Striding hot storm we come tenting our courage and
   hope
With the hope and the courage of the men of America
   Europe Australia and all the sea islands
The good men the true men the strong men the working
   men
Whose sweat is their daily bread whose strength is their
   class
Scientists craftsmen teachers painters poets philosophers
   come
We shall work till our power invested together create a
   new world

Till there be no longer famine in India
Till the Yangtes floods no more
Till we plant gardens in Gobi
Till we gather each year the harvest of the Sahara
Till our force bright as the atom blasts the evil
   oppression which cripples all our creations

And so, I rest the little blond German child gently
     against me
I trace the years with him I rest the little black African
     child gently against me
He and the German boy trace the years with me
I rest the little Kamchatchuan child, gently against me
I rest the little Georgian child gently against me
She and the little Japanese boy trace the years with me
Let our love hold them till bright as the atom together
Their power blasts the evil oppression which cripples all
     our creation
Till man cover the earth with his glory as the waters
     cover the sea.

For a Working Woman

Frances Moore

Honour your hands, my comrade, scarred and worn
by cleaning after, labouring for sons.
White hands as frail and fair as lilies scorn
that scarce have served a useful purpose once.

Honour them with those millions of hands
that hew and heave and plough and weave and make
our life's necessities in all earth's lands.
but little enough for their own needs can take.

Wonderful human hands whose labours wring
fair cities and harvest out of wilderness.
carve beauty from raw stone, make catgut sing
and men's wild dreams in sober deeds express.

Notes for My Son

Alex Comfort

Remember when you hear them beginning to say Freedom
Look carefully — see who it is that they want you to
    butcher.

Remember, when you say that the old trick would not have
    fooled you for a moment
That every time it is the trick which seems new.

Remember that you will have to put in irons
Your better nature, if it will desert to them.

Remember, remember their faces — watch them carefully:
For every step you take is on somebody's body

And every cherry you plant for them is a gibbet
And every furrow you turn for them is a grave.

Remember, the smell of burning will not sicken you
If they persuade you that it will thaw the world.

Beware. The blood of a child does not smell so bitter
If you have shed it with a high moral purpose.

So that because the woodcutter disobeyed
they will not burn her today or any day

So that for lack of a joiner's obedience
the crucifixion will not now take place

So that when they come to sell you their bloody corruption
you will gather the spit of your chest
and plant it in their faces.

148

Know Thy Enemy

Christopher Logue

Know thy enemy:
he does not care what colour you are
provided you work for him
   and yet you do!
he does not care how much you earn
provided you earn more for him
   and yet you do!
he does not care who lives in the room at the top
provided he owns the building
   and yet you strive!
he will let you write against him
provided you do not act against him
   and yet you write!
he sings the praises of humanity
but knows machines cost more than men.
Bargain with him, he laughs, and beats you at it;
challenge him, and he kills.
Sooner than lose the things he owns
he will destroy the world.
SMASH CAPITAL NOW!

Snipers

Roger McGough

When I was kneehigh to a tabletop,
Uncle Ted came home from Burma.
He was the youngest of seven brothers
so the street borrowed extra bunting
and whitewashed him a welcome.

All the relations made the pilgrimage,
including us, laughed, sang, made a fuss.
He was brown as a chairleg,
drank tea out of a white mug the size of my head
and said next to nowt.

But every few minutes he would scan
the ceiling nervously hands begin to shake.
'For snipers', everyone later agreed,
'A difficult habit to break'.

Sometimes when the two of us were alone,
he'd have a snooze after dinner
and I'd keep an eye open for Japs.
Of course, he didn't know this
and the tanner he'd give me before I went
was for keeping quiet,
but I liked to think it was money well spent.

Being Uncle Ted's secret bodyguard
had it's advantages, the pay was good
and the hours were short, but even so,
the novelty soon wore off, and instead,
I started school and became an infant.

Later, I learnt that he was in a mental home.
'Needn't tell anybody... Nothing serious...
Delayed shock... Usual sort of thing
... Completely cured now the doctors say'.
The snipers came down from the ceiling
but they didn't go away.

Over the next five years they picked off
three of his brothers; one of whom was my father.
No glory, no citations,
Bang! straight through the heart.

Uncle Ted's married now, with a family.
He doesn't say much, but each night after tea,
he still dozes fitfully in his favourite armchair.
He keeps out of the sun, and listens now and then
for the tramp tramp of the Colonel Bogeymen.
He knows damn well he's still at war,
just that the snipers aren't Japs anymore.

Mother the Wardrobe is Full of Infantrymen

Roger McGough

mother the wardrobe is full of infantrymen
i did i asked them
but they snarled saying it was a mans life

mother there is a centurion tank in the parlour
i did i asked the officer
but he laughed saying 'Queens regulations'
(piano was out of tune anyway)

mother polish your identity bracelet
there is a mushroom cloud in the backgarden
i did i tried to bring in the cat
but it simply came to pieces in my hand
i did i tried to white-wash the windows
but there weren't any
i did i tried to hide under the stairs
but i couldn't get in for civil defence leaders
i did i tried to ring candid camera
but they crossed their hearts

i went for a policeman but they were looting the town
i went for a fire engine but they were all upside down
i went for a priest but they were all on their knees
mother don't just lie there say something please
mother don't just lie there say something please

The Gaudy Camp Follower

Jack Beeching

She took her scarlet knickers off
To wave them at the sailors
And that was when we mutineers
Decided to be failures.

Her face was paint and varnish,
Her smile a cheerful grin.
Most of us called her Freedom,
But some, Original Sin.

She waved her scarlet banner
At the drunkard and the rebel
Who dreamed that all they'd dreamed of
Was needed, and was noble.

She opened wide her aperture,
Wide enough to swallow us.
We ran into her trap like mice
And there were more to follow us.

She took us in when we were boys,
And, now our hair is grey,
After a lifetime in her lap
How can we get away?

Too many years spent spending,
How can we start to save?
A lifetime in that succulent pit
And one foot in the grave.

Sudden Discords in the Trumpets of Overdelayed Last Judgement, 1956

Jack Lindsay

We were looking another way
when the bomb blew up the bridge,
blew up all bridges, it seemed.
We stood in abject dismay
on an island of devastation.
All familiar shapes were dimmed,
twisted. In consternation
we took out our maps, but the roads
had changed their names and directions.
The imposing landmarks were gone.

For a while we wandered on,
with no one to answer our questions.
Our calls had no echoes. At last
we halted in huddling fear
as winds from all quarters blustered.

In the endless night I dreamed
that my own Face came near
from the other end of space.
grinning, unscarred, ungrieving.
'You knew it all,' my Voice said,
'I'm the one you'll never deceive.
Don't lie any more or you're damned'
to the dingiest ditches of hell.'

'I knew nothing,' I weakly replied.

I knew nothing. And yet you knew,
you blandly assert. You could tell
the insidious lies from the true.

My otherself said with a sneer,
'Dialectical insight you claimed,
but never once grasped, it's quite clear,
the deep nature of contradictions,
the darkness, the guile there, as well
as the obvious opposites clashing.

Only a child could believe
that life with loud cheers would advance
on such a straightforward track.
Laired in paradise regained
is the subtly satanic curse.'

'I'm lost, I've no compass, no guide.'
'Then there's some hope. You must pierce
to the core of the moving whole
with its tangle of choice and of chance,
its shrouded and shining goal.
Now cast all illusions aside,
but reject disillusionment too.'

I woke in the sudden morning
with stormclouds luridly spread.
The road was there, baffled and torn,
glimpsed and then brokenly lost,
with all ditches and dangers crisscrossed
in its zigzag towards the unknown.

Yet I saw how it led on ahead.
I saw there was no turning-back.
I was one of a host, and alone.
Alone, I was one of a host.

Confessions of an Old Believer

Wisdom comes of disillussionment
Santayana

Jim Burns

It was 1945
I was nine years old
and full of enthusiasm
for our gallant Russian allies.
SECOND FRONT NOW was scrawled
in foot-high letters
on the air-raid shelter in the street,
and along a gable wall
were the words, SUPPORT THE CP.
On VE Day everyone hung out Union Jacks
apart from my Uncle Stan
who had a Hammer & Sickle
outside his bedroom window.

In the nearby cinema
they played the National Anthem
at the end of each programme,
but followed it quickly
with The Cossack Patrol,
and I knew which was more exciting
as visions of snow
and The People's Army
came swirling into my mind.
After all, wasn't it Stalin himself
who'd concocted the recipe
for Uncle Joe's Mint Balls,
and so guaranteed to keep us all aglow?

There was something in the air.
I saw Harry Pollitt plain
and watched Willie Gallacher on a street corner,

speaking to a small crowd.
He was flush-faced and fat
and wore a shabby, belted raincoat.

The local Labour Club
was at the end of our street,
and it wasn't what I really wanted,
but I collected numbers
outside the Polling Station.
They gave me a hot-pot supper
and five shillings,
and I knew I'd been compromised.

I held on until 1948.
Masaryk fell from a window in Prague,
there were rumblings around Berlin.
By 1950 it was almost over.
Iron Curtain, spies, Korea, strikes,
everything had gone badly wrong.
I sat on the edge of the pavement,
my feet in the gutter.
watching the dirty rain water
trickling over my scuffed shoes,
and sneaking longing looks
at the well-spoken, uniformed girls
on their way to the Convent School.

I knew things could never be the same,
and in any case the Party
would not accept my discovery of be-bop,
that decadent American music.
The air-raid shelters had long since disappeared,
and the words on the gable wall
were faded and and almost unreadable.
I tore up my commitment,
tossed the pieces in the air,
and watched them scatter in the cold wind.

How Can
We Sleep?

To My Fellow Artists

Christopher Logue

I

Today, it came to me. How you, my friends
who write, who draw and carve,
friends who make pictures, act, direct,
finger delicate instruments,
compose, or fake, or criticise — how,
in the oncoming megaton bombardments,
all you stand for will be gone
like an arrow into hell.

II

It is strange, and yet
if I tell you how the sunlight glitters
off intricate visions etched into breastplates
by Trojan smiths, you say: Yes! Yes!
And if I say:
around my bedposts birds have built their nests
that sing: No! No! —
or say: when I flog salt, it rains;
when I sell flour, it blows —
you feel my hopelessness; and more,
you understand my words.

But if I speak straight out, and say:
infatuates to local immortality,
distinguished each from each by baby pains
you measure against baby pain, you stand
to lose the earth, and look alike
as if you spat each other out, you say:
Logue grinds his axe again. He's red —
or cashing in... And you are right:
I have an axe to grind. Compared to you,
I'm red and short of cash. So what?
I think, am weak, need help, must live,

161

and will — with your permission — live.
Why should I seek to puzzle you with words
when your beds are near sopping with blood?
And yet I puzzle you with words.

III

If (as many of you do) you base
all of your hope, all of that hope
necessary to make a work of art
on unborn generations, start
hunting for a place to hide the art
you will create in privation.

Consider, my fellows,
how all the posh goodies inside our museums,
stones, books, things we have stolen,
think of them turned to instant dust
one dusk between six and six-ten.

It is true: they will say you are fools
who know nothing of politics.
Women and artists must keep out of politics.
They will suggest (politely... politely...)
that the length of your hair pre-empts your sanity.
They will, with their reasons,
prove your unreasonableness;
though you are drugged by rationality.

They will do all in their power
(and their power is great)
to shut you up, until
recommending your wife's sensual niceties,
or lamenting her, loose in the hilts
you thrive like milestones for whom
the Queen's green £s were contagious.

IV

Listen, I beg you. Six days ago
a paper called *The Sunday Times*
revealed, with witless candour,
their dead thoughts:

You are confused about destruction, yes?

they said. and then — recommending the death of the
    country
in the name of the country: *We shall bomb,*
if bomb we must, bomb like King Billy
for the British have something to die for.
No mention was made of something to live for.
Saying (in the names of loyalty, faith, integrity):
How vile are they who wish to live here
minus the local notion of democracy

Not speaking of those who wish to die here.

The death before dishonour, boys;
the death before gestapo, boys;
the death before a tyrant, boys;
the death before *The Sunday Times*.

But where is the dishonour, gestapo, or tyrant?
And who wants to dishonour or govern a cinder?
My friends,
how difficult it is for those who speak
out of anger to answer those who speak
out of complacency.

And yet, imagine a horror
and perpetrate horrors because of it,
is called mad.

Think desolation
and create desolation because of it,
is called mad.
Thus they think of our country.

So do you agree with them
Spender, and Barker, and Auden?
And you my newly married master, Eliot —
will you adopt their lie by silence
and having sold our flesh to war
bequeath our bones to God?
Or are there two sides to *this* question?

But I fear we are easily beaten.
So where shall we hide them, our treasures?
Uncertain the disused chalk pit;
uncertain the bank's steel vault:
and the holds of ships are uncertain.

We must beg for permission
to hang our paintings underground,
to store our books and stones in mines;
but the rents will be high underground,
and I doubt if we can afford them.

Perhaps they will let a few of us hide
in the negative silos, 1000 feet down,
where, beside telephones, uniformed men
await fatal words.
We must not be afraid to ask;
for works concerning the private heart
will not alter devoted experts.

But let us remember to leave behind
permanent signs. Signs that are easily read.
Signs that say: So deep,
beneath so many feet of stone,
is a poem expressing refinement of taste,
a book about logic, a tape of quartets,
and a picture of the painter's wife.

Then can our six-handed grandsons,
our unborn consolation,
discover that we too, had art.
And those who dare look
over the crater's jagged rim,
may, in the evening, climb down
into the mauve bowl of London,
and dig.
While their guards watch out
for tyrants and food, and sun.

Think, men of no future,
but with a name to come.

A War Memoir
on finding Spike Milligan's oddly incomplete

Arnold Rattenbury

I knew a man who could only love
To the sound of brass band music. He was in luck,
For there was much about those days. The shove
Of trombones must have told him Fuck.

And one I knew thought it his duty,
In view of the paper shortage, to shit one turd
A day, a dry one — known, fondly, as Beauty —
To save on wiping afterward.

Another took a girl to bed
But couldn't make anything useful happen at all
On the flat like that, who'd learnt his loving instead
Up against the canteen wall.

And a Regular we filled with beer
To hear the National Anthem blow from his arse
As far as the notes for 'Glorious': loud, clear,
And learnt indeed up the Khyber Pass.

Never before or since have I
Been privy to such strange confidence in squads
Of bodies, kitted in uniform's utter lie.
(One man believed his body God's).

But there were other differences
Then. The whole extraordinary lot was at war.
Myself and the five I have mentioned for instances
Knew why, and which Class we were for.

No More Hiroshimas

James Kirkup

At the station exit, my bundle in hand,
Early the winter afternoon's wet snow
Falls thinly round me, out of a crudded sun.
I had forgotten to remember where I was.
Looking about, I see it might be anywhere —
A station, a town like any other in Japan,
Ramshackle, muddy, noisy, drab; a cheerfully
Shallow permanence: peeling concrete, litter, 'Atomic
Lotion, for hair fall-out', a flimsy department-store;
Racks and towers of neon, flashy over tiled and tilted waves
Of little roofs, shacks cascading lemons and persimmons,
Oranges and dark-red apples, shanties awash with rainbows
Of squid and octopus, shellfish, slabs of tuna, oysters, ice,
Ablaze with fans of soiled nude-picture books
Thumbed abstractedly by schoolboys, with second-hand
    looks.

The river remains unchanged, sad, refusing rehabilitation.
In this long, wide, empty official boulevard
The new trees are still small, the office blocks
Basely functional, the bridge a slick abstraction.
But the river remains unchanged, sad, refusing
    rehabilitation.

In the city centre, far from the station's lively squalor,
A kind of life goes on, in cinemas and hi-fi coffee bars,
In the shuffling racket of pin-table palaces and parlours,
The souvenir-shops piled with junk, kimonoed kewpie-dolls,

Models of the bombed Industry Promotion Hall, memorial
    ruin
Tricked out with glitter-frost and artificial pearls.

Set in an awful emptiness, the modern tourist hotel is
    trimmed
With jaded Christmas frippery, flatulent balloons; in the
    hall,
A giant dingy iced cake in the shape of a Cinderella coach.
The contemporary stairs are treacherous, the corridors
Deserted, my room an overheated morgue, the bar in
    darkness.
Punctually, the electric chimes ring out across the tidy
    waste
Their doleful public hymn the tune unrecognizable,
    evangelist.

Here atomic peace is geared to meet the tourist trade.
Let it remain like this, for all the world to see,
Without nobility or loveliness, and dogged with shame
That is beyond all hope of indignation. Anger, too, is dead.
And why should memorials of what was far
From pleasant have the grace that helps us to forget?
In the dying afternoon, I wander dying round the Park of
    Peace.
It is right, this squat, dead place, with its left-over air
Of an abandoned International Trade and Tourist Fair.
The stunted trees are wrapped in straw against the cold.
The gardeners are old, old women in blue bloomers, white
    aprons,
Survivors weeding the dead brown lawns around the
    Children's Monument.

A hideous pile, the Atomic Bomb Explosion Centre, freezing
    cold,
'Includes the Peace Tower, a museum containing
Atomic-melted slates and bricks, photos showing
What the Atomic Desert looked like, and other
Relics of the catastrophe.'

The other relics:
The ones that made me weep;
The bits of burnt clothing,
The stopped watches, the torn shirts.
The twisted buttons,
The stained and tattered vests and drawers,
The ripped kimonos and charred boots,
The white blouse polka-dotted with atomic rain, indelible,
The cotton summer pants the blasted boys crawled home
    in, to bleed
And slowly die.

Remember only these.
They are the memorials we need.

Latest News

David Craig

They are turning people into hulks of mud.
His hair plastered, clothes messed
To soiled anonymous scraps —
Her shirt and skin and hair
One scab of puddled brown — they stare
At nothing in the world but the point of the knife.

They have abused every common thing —
A knife, water, wire, a jar.
They stick the wire through hands and cheeks —
'You gotta see how quiet dem gooks sit
When we gottem wrapped up like dat.'
They shove them down in the water till they choke,
Throw them out of the helicopters,
Drag them through the paddy tied to a truck.

Unanswered questions, anger at the heat —
These are the latest reasons
For turning a person into a hulk of mud.
Can we sit here any longer
While our own kind choke on swallowed blood?
How can we sleep?

The easiest thing in the world, to eat and sleep —
Our eyelids aren't burnt off, we still have tongues.

It has happened somewhere every year
Since I was young.
I will write about something else
When the torturers have been stopped.
Then it will be natural to study
Or sing an unworried song.

To Whom It May Concern
(Tell Me Lies about Vietnam)

Adrian Mitchell

I was run over by the truth one day.
Ever since the accident I've walked this way.
  So stick my legs in plaster
  Tell me lies about Vietnam.

Heard the alarm clock screaming with pain,
Couldn't find myself so I went back to sleep again
  So fill my ears with silver
  Stick my legs in plaster
  Tell me lies about Vietnam.

Every time I shut my eyes all I see is flames.
Made a marble phone book and I carved all the names
  So coat my eyes with butter
  Fill my ears with silver
  Stick my legs in plaster
  Tell me lies about Vietnam.

I smell something burning, hope it's just my brains.
They're only dropping peppermints and daisy-chains
  So stuff my nose with garlic
  Coat my eyes with butter
  Fill my ears with silver
  Stick my legs in plaster
  Tell me lies about Vietnam.

Where were you at the time of the crime?
Down by the Cenotaph drinking slime
　So chain my tongue with whisky
　Stuff my nose with garlic
　Coat my eyes with butter
　Fill my ears with silver
　Stick my legs in plaster
　Tell me lies about Vietnam.

You put your bombers in, you put your conscience out,
You take the human being and you twist it all about
　So scrub my skin with women
　Chain my tongue with whisky
　Stuff my nose with garlic
　Coat my eyes with butter
　Fill my ears with silver
　Stick my legs in plaster
　Tell me lies about Vietnam.

Victor Jara of Chile

Adrian Mitchell

Victor Jara of Chile
Lived like a shooting star
He fought for the people of Chile
With his songs and his guitar

And his hands were gentle
His hands were strong

Victor Jara was a peasant
Worked from a few years old
He sat upon his father's plough
And watched the earth unfold

And his hands were gentle
His hands were strong

When the neighbours had a wedding
Or one of their children died
His mother sang all night for them
With Victor by her side

And his hands were gentle
His hands were strong

He grew to be fighter
Against the people's wrongs
He listened to their grief and joy
And turned them into songs

And his hands were gentle
His hands were strong

He sang about the copper miners
And those who work the land
He sang about the factory workers
And they knew he was their man

And his hands were gentle
His hands were strong

He campaigned for Allende
Working night and day
He sang: take hold of your brother's hand
The future begins today

And his hands were gentle
His hands were strong

The bloody generals seized Chile
They arrested Victor then
They caged him in a stadium
With five thousand frightened men

And his hands were gentle
His hands were strong

Victor stood in the stadium
His voice was brave and strong
He sang for his fellow-prisoners
Till the guards cut short his song

And his hands were gentle
His hands were strong

They broke the bones in both his hands
They beat his lovely head
They tore him with electric shocks
After two long days of torture they shot him dead

And his hands were gentle
His hands were strong

And now the Generals rule Chile
And the British have their thanks
For they rule with Hawker Hunters
And they rule with Chieftain tanks

And his hands were gentle
His hands were strong

Victor Jara of Chile
Lived like a shooting star
He fought for the people of Chile
With his songs and his guitar

And his hands were gentle
His hands were strong

This ballad has been set to music and recorded by Arlo Guthrie

Homage to Salvador Allende

'Our enemies have beat us to the pit:
It is more worthy to leap in ourselves,
Than tarry till they push us...'
Brutus at Philippi

E.P. Thompson

Well, comrade president, what is there left to say?
Predicted all the way: and buried in the end
Without the benefit of media, before the mass
Could say its newses over you, the cameras
Squat in your wounds and blow them up.

Failure makes you like us, our kind of man,
Killed by our kind: petrol pump patriots;
Loyal executives; most loyal constitutional ladies,
Wed to destroyers, setters-on of jets;
Our kindly patient partner, General Fabius,
Who when he strikes strikes hard, getting us in the guts.
Your face was too much common. Money fled uphill
And cost them in their lives who cost your death.

Your art was always an impossible.
Couldn't you learn, with less than half the votes,
The prose of power, the public man's inflation?
You should have been our age, trading their terms
For something less than half a treachery...

Defective realist, poor loyal sod,
Old silly doctor in a palace on your own,
Knowing the odds were up —
                              Why do you hurt our hearts?

Poetic, Latin man! You do not fall within
Our frames of reference. Transfixed by promises
Pledged to the poor in the high Andean pastures;

176

The crowd in Santiago; the clasped hand of the metal-
    worker;
The earnest village schoolmistress, searching your face:
These brought their treaties. You signed them with your life

Which you trade now into myth's ageless reference:
Bolivar, Guevara, Allende. Generous continent!
Accusing hemisphere! But not our kind of men,
As we, back in our prosing beds, stir in our myths,
Recalling such men once... and at Philippi one
Who, having fought and failed, took on a Roman end.

September, 1973

Remember Haiti, Cuba, Vietnam

Andrew Salkey

Here's something folk tales tell
us about, at night, but which
we lose sight of during the day:

Giants can be surprised.

That's something three slingshots
in our third of the world gauged
and defiantly stretched to success.

What's the light like now in the dark?

Look at the untouched stones
lying on our beaches
and the idle rubber bands
in our upturned hands!

Clearsightedness
(In memory of Claudia Jones)

Andrew Salkey

In spite of what the quarrymen said,
she was sure she knew only too well
that she was born to see through stone,
to slash that broad back with her eyes
and tell her daughter about it, one day.

I remember we'd often catch her smiling,
brushing rock-dust out of her hair,
clapping her granite-veined hands,
slapping her long skirt with carpet-clatter,
and looking like a moving hive of hillside.

Fantasy of an African Boy

James Berry

Such a peculiar lot
we are, we people
without money, in daylong
yearlong sunlight, knowing
money is somewhere, somewhere.

Everybody says it's a big
bigger brain bother now,
money. Such millions and millions
of us don't manage at all
without it, like war going on.

And we can't eat it. Yet
without it our heads alone
stay big, as lots and lots do,
coming from nowhere joyful,
going nowhere happy.

We can't drink it up. Yet
without it we shrivel when small
and stop for ever
where we stopped,
as lots and lots do.

We can't read money for books.
Yet without it we don't
read, don't write numbers.
don't open gates in other countries,
as lots and lots never do.

We can't use money to bandage
sores, can't pound it
to powder for sick eyes
and sick bellies. Yet without
it flesh melts from our bones.

Such walled-round gentlemen
overseas minding money! Such
bigtime gentlemen, body guarded
because of too much respect
and too many wishes on them:

too many wishes, everywhere,
wanting them to let go
magic of money, and let it fly
away everywhere, day and night,
just like dropped leaves in wind!

Starting to Make a Tree

Roy Fisher

First we carried out the faggot of steel stakes; they
varied in length, though most were taller than a man.

We slid one free of the bundle and drove it into the
ground, first padding the top with rag, that the branch
might not be injured with leaning on it.

Then we took turns to choose stakes of the length we
wanted, and to feel for the distances between them. We
gathered to thrust them firmly in.

There were twenty or thirty of them in all; and when
they were in place we had, round the clearing we had left
for the trunk, an irregular radial plantation of these
props, each with its wad of white at the tip. It was to be
an old, downcurving tree.

This was in keeping with the burnt, chemical blue of the
soil, and the even hue of the sky which seemed to have
been washed with a pale brownish smoke;

another clue was the flatness of the horizon on all sides
except the north, where it was broken by the low slate or
tarred shingle roofs of the houses, which stretched away
from us for a mile or more.

This was the work of the morning. It was done with care,
for we had no wish to make revisions;

we were, nonetheless, a little excited, and hindered the
women at their cooking in our anxiety to know whose
armpit and whose groin would help us most in the
modelling of the bole, and the thrust of the boughs.

That done, we spent the early dusk of the afternoon gathering materials from the nearest houses; and there was plenty:

a great flock mattress; two carved chairs; cement; chicken-wire; tarpaulin; a smashed barrel; lead piping; leather of all kinds; and many small things.

In the evening we sat late, and discussed how we could best use them. Our tree was to be very beautiful.

On the Closing of Millom Ironworks

September 1968

Norman Nicholson

Wandering by the heave of the town park, wondering
Which way the day will drift,
On the spur of a habit I turn to the feathered
Weathercock of the furnace chimneys.
                                But no grey smoke-tail
Pointers the mood of the wind. The hum
And blare that for a hundred years
Drummed at the town's deaf ears
Now fills the air with the roar of its silence.
They'll need no more to swill the slag-dust off the
    windows;
The curtains will be cleaner
And the grass plots greener
Round the Old Folk's council flats. The tanged autumnal
    mist
Is filtered free of soot and sulphur,
And the wind blows in untainted.
It's beautiful to breathe the sharp night air.
But, morning after morning, there
They stand, by the churchyard gate,
Hands in pockets, shoulders to the slag,
The men whose fathers stood there back in '28,
When their sons were at school with me.
                                The town
Rolls round the century's bleak orbit.
                            Down
On the ebb-tide sands, the five-funneled
Battleship of the furnace lies beached and rusting;
Run aground, not floundered;
Not a crack in her hull;
Lacking but a loan to float her off.

184

The Market

Square is busy as the men file by
To sign on at the 'Brew'. But not a face
Tilts upward, no one enquires of the sky.
The smoke prognosticates no how
Or why of any practical tomorrow.
For what does it matter if it rains all day?
And what's the good of knowing
Which way the wind is blowing
When whichever way it blows it's a cold wind now.

The *Brew* or *Broo*: the Labour Exchange

Workers in Metal

E.J. Scovell

Working surely overtime, the scaffolders
Against the evening sky of early winter
With their skill's panache and the dissonant music of metal
Between tall houses raise their handsome structure,
And now itself it has taken on the tone
Of age, because the builders not the next
Nor any day the winter through returned.

Well, we are in their hands who are at home
With metal, whether it may be the bold
Against the sky night-faring scaffolders;
Or dreamers of machines for peace and war;
Or those who in the chairman's room
Dispose the imaginary gold.

Glasgow Sonnets

Edwin Morgan

i

A mean wind wanders through the backcourt trash.
Hackles on puddles rise, old mattresses
puff briefly and subside. Play-fortresses
of brick and bric-a-brac spill out some ash.
Four storeys have no windows left to smash,
but in the fifth a chipped sill buttresses
mother and daughter the last mistresses
of that black block condemned to stand, not crash.
Around them the cracks deepen, the rats crawl.
The kettle whimpers on a crazy hob.
Roses of mould grow from ceiling to wall.
The man lies late since he has lost his job,
smokes on one elbow, letting his coughs fall
thinly into an air too poor to rob.

ii

A shilpit dog fucks grimly by the close.
Late shadows lengthen slowly, slogans fade.
The YY PARTICK TOI grins from its shade
like the last strains of some lost *libera nos
a malo*. No deliverer ever rose
from these stone tombs to get the hell they made
unmade. The same weans never make the grade.
The same grey street sends back the ball it throws.
Under the darkness of a twisted pram
a cat's eyes glitter. Glittering stars press
between the silent chimney-cowls and cram
the higher spaces with their SOS.
Don't shine a torch on the ragwoman's dram.
Coats keep the evil cold out less and less.

iii

'See a tenement due for demolition?
I can get ye rooms in it, two, okay?
Seven hundred and nothin legal to pay
for it's no legal, see? That's my proposition,
ye can take it or leave it but. The position
is simple, you want a hoose, I say
for eight hundred pound it's yours.' And they
trailing five bairns, accepted his omission
of the foul crumbling stairwell, windows wired
not glazed, the damp from the canal, the cooker
without pipes, packs of rats that never tired —
any more than the vandals bored with snooker
who stripped the neighbouring houses, howled, and fired
their aerosols — of squeaking 'Filthy lucre!'

iv

Down by the brickworks you get warm at least.
Surely soup-kitchens have gone out? It's not
the Thirties now. Hugh MacDiarmid forgot
in 'Glasgow 1960' that the feast
of reason and the flow of soul has ceased
to matter to the long unfinished plot
of heating frozen hands. We never got
an abstruse song that charmed the raging beast.
So you have nothing to lose but your chains,
dear Seventies. Dalmarnock, Maryhill,
Blackhill and Govan, better sticks and stanes
should break your banes, for poets' words are ill
to hurt ye. On the wrecker's ball the rains
of greeting cities drop and drink their fill.

v

'Let them eat cake' made no bones about it.
But we say let them eat the hope deferred
and that will sicken them. We have preferred
silent slipways to the riveters' wit.
And don't deny it — that's the ugly bit.

Ministers' tears might well have launched a herd
of bucking tankers if they'd been transferred
from Whitehall to the Clyde. And smiles don't fit
either. 'There'll be no bevvying' said Reid
at the work-in. But all the dignity you muster
can only give you back a mouth to feed
and rent to pay if what you lose in bluster
is no more than win patience with 'I need'
while distant blackboards use you as their duster.

vi

The North Sea oil-strike tilts east Scotland up,
and the great sick Clyde shivers in its bed.
But elegists can't hang themselves on fled-
from trees or poison a recycled cup —
If only a less faint, shaky sunup
glimmered through the skeletal shop and shed
and men washed round the piers like gold and spread
golder in soul than Mitsubishi or Krupp —
The images are ageless but the thing
is now. Without my images the men
ration their cigarettes, their children cling
to broken toys, their women wonder when
the doors will bang on laughter and a wing
over the firth be simply joy again.

vii

Environmentalists, ecologists
and conservationists are fine no doubt.
Pedestrianization will come out
fighting, riverside walks march off the lists,
pigeons and starlings be somnambulists
in far-off suburbs, the sandblaster's grout
multiply pink piebald facades to pout
at sticky-fingered mock-Venetianists.
Prop up's the motto. Splint the dying age.
Never displease the watchers from the grave.
Great when fake architecture was the rage,

but greater still to see what you can save.
The gutted double fake meets the adage:
a wig's the thing to beat both beard and shave.

viii

Meanwhile the flyovers breed loops of light
in curves that would have ravished tragic Toshy —
clean and unpompous, nothing wishy-washy.
Vistas swim out from the bulldozer's bite
by day, and banks of earthbound stars at night
begin. In Madame Emé's Sauchie Haugh, she
could never gain in leaves or larks or sploshy
lanes what's lost in a dead boarded site —
the life that overspill is overkill to.
Less is not more, and garden cities are
the flimsiest oxymoron to distil to.
And who wants to distil? Let bus and car
and hurrying umbrellas keep their skill to
feed ukiyo-e beyond Lochnagar.

ix

It groans and shakes, contracts and grows again.
Its giant broken shoulders shrug off rain.
It digs its pits to a shauchling refrain.
Roadworks and graveyards like their gallus men.
It fattens fires and murders in a pen
and lets them out in flaps and squalls of pain.
It sometimes tears its smoky counterpane
to hoist a bleary fist at nothing, then
at everything, you never know. The west
could still be laid with no one's tears like dust
and barricaded windows be the best
to see from till the shops, the ships, the trust
return like thunder. Give the Clyde the rest.
Man and the sea make cities as they must.

From thirtieth floor windows at Red Road
he can see choughs and samphires, dreadful trade —
the schoolboy reading *Lear* has that scene made.
A multi is a sonnet stretched to ode
and some say that's no joke. The gentle load
of souls in clouds, vertiginously stayed
above the windy courts, is probed and weighed.
Each monolith stands patient, ah'd and oh'd.
And stalled lifts generating high-rise blues
can be set loose. But stalled lives never budge.
They linger in the single-ends that use
their spirit to the bone, and when they trudge
from closemouth to laundrette their steady shoes
carry a world that weighs us like a judge.

Ballad of the Two Left Hands

Douglas Dunn

When walking out one morning
  Walking down Clydeside Street
I met a man with two left hands
  Who said he was obsolete.

At noon the work horns sounded through
  The shipyards on Clyde's shore
And told men that the day had come
  When they'd work there no more.

Economy is hand and sweat
  A welder in his mask
A new apprentice pouring tea.
  From his father's thermos flask.

And soon these men of several trades
  Stood there on Clydeside Street
Stood staring at each new left hand
  That made them obsolete.

'Beware of men in suits', one said
  'Take it from me, it's true
Their drivel economics'll
  Put two left hands on you.'

All in the afternoon was shut
  When I walked out again
The day had pulled on its black gloves
  And turned its back on men.

I walked the dusk of darkened cranes
  Clyde broke on Clyde's dark shore
And rivets fired where men still work
  Though men work here no more.

High in the night's dark universe
  I saw the promised star
That men I knew raise glasses to
  In an illegal bar.

They toast that city still to come
  Where truth and justice meet
And though they don't know where it is
  It's not on Clydeside Street.

With thumbs stuck on the wrong way round
  In two left-footed shoes
I saw a man search in his heart,
  And ask it, 'Are you true?'

That man who sat on Clydeside Street
  Looked up at me and said
'I'll study this, then I'll pick clean
  The insides of my head.'

And moonlight washed the shipyards then
  Each crane was hung with stars
Rinsed in the moonlight we stared up
  Like old astronomers.

Economy is hand and sweat
  And foundrymen and fire
Revise your textbook, multiply
  Your guilt by your desire.

Such dignity, so many lives,
  Even on Clydeside Street
'When mind and heart together ask
  'Why are we obsolete?'

Jarrow

Carol Rumens

Nothing is left to dig, little to make:
Night has engulfed both firelit hall and sparrow.
Wind and car-noise pour across the Slake.
Nothing is left to dig, little to make
A stream of rust where a great ship might grow.
And where a union-man was hung for show
Nothing is left to dig, little to make.
Night has engulfed both firelit hall and sparrow.

Glasgow Schoolboys, Running Backwards

Douglas Dunn

High wind... They turn their backs to it, and push.
Their crazy strides are chopped in little steps.
And all their lives, like that, they'll have to rush
Forwards in reverse, always holding their caps.

Women in the Cold War

Alison Fell

Outside, time and famous dates passed –
Korea Suez Cuba Algeria all cannoned by
casually as a slap on the back.
In the butcher's and the grocer's,
not a word of them. No, only talk of
the sun, snow, seasons;
stillbirths, new banns posted;
the harvest, the Gala,
the Foot and Mouth which closed farm roads,
the Compensation.
As for violence, we had our own —
a thousand cattle burned in pits
a labourer, demented, raped a child
fine swimmers drowned in the loch's depths.
And most Saturdays some girl's wedding
brought the women clattering
down the High Street — they'd bang
on doors along the way and put up the cry,
then hang back respectfully and squint
at the hired cars, the ceremonial clothes.
My mother, her mother's mother
were brides like these,
country brides teetering up
the gravel-chipped path to the Kirk,
shielding their new shoes from scrapes.
By the sandstone wall, photos were posed,
against a bleak swell of lowland hills;
the photos show puckered faces
and a wind which whips the stiff bouquets.
The dances came and went, and fashions;
my girlfriends and I —in tight skirts
(or tiered), beads which popped
and hooped net petticoats —

crushed into cars and choked
on our own close scent, and smoke, and compliments.
But soon they sobered and they planned —
knitted cardigans all summer, by January
scanned the catalogues for cottons,
drab (for work), dressy (for holidays).
I saw them smooth
and full-blown dreaming of marriage
when I was still pockmarked with envy
and a thousand wants. I became crazy:
'I'll be an artist' I said
and bristled for the skirmish; quite slowly
their eyes scaled and their good sense
bunched against me.
'That's no' for the likes o' us.'
Elizabeth, Elaine, Rhoda of the long legs,
all matrons, mothering, hurrying
their men to work at 7am.
Now hunched round prams,
what landmarks of content do they stake out
as the village circles?
As tractors streak the fields with lime
and all the old women, hushed,
move to the funeral to see the flowers.

Enduring
on the Barricades

The 1984 Tour of Britain

Ken Smith

Miners hunted down the corn by the mounted division.
Sad poverty's lament around the garden festival.
There's work in nuclear construction and security.
And yet much bitterness in the land of the butter
    mountain.
Sad junketing around the wine lakes. And here
the missiles we can't see move in their circles
on a page deleted in the interest of national security
while we were standing round in groups of one or less.
But we shall build Jerusalem. Well worth a visit.

Twenty Million Buckets

Bert Ward

There he stands with his bucket
Collecting money for the miners
Against all the resources of the State.

There they stand with their buckets
The pair of them
Collecting money for the miners
Against all the resources of the State.

There they stand with their buckets
The four of them
Collecting money for the miners
Against all the resources of the State.

There they stand with their buckets
A million of them
Collecting money for the miners
Against all the resources of the State.

There they stand with their buckets
Twenty millions of them
Collecting money for the miners
Against all the resources of the State.

And there she stands
With all the resources of the State
Against twenty million buckets.

---

*Written while collecting for the miners, in Sydenham, during
the Great Strike. Bert Ward was then secretary of the local
Communist Party branch.*

Redundant Miners

Mogg Williams

They coughed into the Aquarius wind,
Spat out fag ends
And street-cornered small talk
About lean hungry streets.

They chatted about the future,
The present, and that, and that,
Of times that had gone,
Half buried in the distant past.

Talk was all they had,
A measurement of busy words
That hugged street corners.
Gloved in the Aquarius wind.

And yet.
Were they ever so true to themselves,
They owned the stars and wandering clouds,
The circling moon and sun
And the north wind blowing south.

A Thatcher

Judith Kazantzis

A thatcher is someone who makes a roof
or used to, when things were quieter,
was someone who sheltered people
from the rain, when things were quieter.
A thatcher took folks from the wind
and layered the skin of a human weather.
Now a thatcher exposes the dwellers,
rips off the roof in the skinning wind,
hurls down the roof on the dwellers,
who for cover snatch at the straws
the roof-maker rains
on their rainwashed heads ruthlessly
and in their teeth and in their eyes
like a war
that the thatcher unnaturally makes
on the dwellers. And the luckier,
snatching more straw cover of the undoing
thatch, despise the unluckier, the colder ones,
so that some see but many don't
or do see but not why, and think it
the way of a brave wise thatcher
that their fellows are icy and cold
in an inhuman country.

Job Hunting

Brian Patten

On the wasteland that stretches
From here to the river
My children play a game.
It is called job hunting.
They blacken their faces,
And with knives and imitation guns
They go stalking among
The lichen-coated ruins
Of broken machinery and cranes.
It is an exciting game.
Sometimes they come back exhausted,
Clutching objects they have prised
From the earth —
Nuts, bolts, the broken vizor
Of a welder's mask.
'Daddy,' they ask, 'Daddy,
Is this a job? Can we keep it?'

Poverty

Julia Darling

you don't see it
it's packed out of town
in houses with no furniture
waiting for cheques that come by post
handed out by the invisible
watched over by shadows
kept in files and case histories
you know it by its bus routes
by what the shops are selling
by lettuce leaves by mushroom stalks
by bargains and poundstretchers
betting shops and lotteries
by well dressed children that cry
by how many seagulls are out looking for food
and how many dogs are out leadless
too many hairdressers
and not enough cafes
by out of date community posters
by social clubs with locks
broken windows with bars
and policeman who stay in their cars
by murals gone faded
sofa beds costing only forty five quid
and people who are friendly
but on their own
who talk as if they know you
and are used to not being heard
by women with babies and no prams
and the men in the park who smoke
and watch toddlers
by women with prams and no babies

National Trust

Tony Harrison

Bottomless pits. There's one in Castleton,
and stout upholders of our law and order
one day thought its depth worth wagering on
and borrowed a convict hush-hush from his warder
and winched him down; and back, flayed, grey, mad, dumb.

Not even a good flogging made him holler!

O gentlemen, a better way to plumb
the depths of Britain's dangling a scholar,
say, here at the booming shaft at Towanroath,
now National Trust, a place where they got tin,
those gentlemen who silenced the men's oath
and killed the language that they swore it in.

The dumb go down in history and disappear
and not one gentleman's been brought to book:

Mes den hep tavas a-gollas y dyr

(Cornish) —

       'the tongueless man gets his land took.'

Sonny's Lettah
Anti-Sus* poem

Linton Kwesi Johnson

Brixtan Prison
Jebb Avenue
Landan South-west two
Inglan

Dear Mama,
Good Day.
I hope dat wen
deze few lines reach yu,
they may find yu in di bes af helt.

Mama,
I really don't know how fi tell yu dis,
cause I did mek a salim pramis
fi tek care a likkle Jim
an try mi bes fi look out fi him.

Mama,
Ah really did try mi bes,
but nondiles
mi sarry fi tell yu seh
pnor likkle Jim get arres.

It woz di miggle a di rush howah
wen evrybady jus a hosle an a bosle
fi goh home fi dem evenin showah;
mi and Jim stan-up
waitin pan a bus,
nat cauzin no fus,
wen all af a sudden
a police van pull-up.

Out jump tree policeman,
di hole a dem carryin batan.
Dem waak straight up to mi an Jim.
One a dem hol awn to Jim
seh him tekin him in;
Jim tell him fi let goh a him
far him noh dhu notn,
an him naw tief,
nat even a butn.
Jim start to wriggle
di police start to giggle.

Mama,
mek I tell yu whe dem dhu to Jim
Mama,
mek I tell yu whe dem dhu to him:

dem tump him in him belly
an it turn to jelly
dem lick him pan him back
an him rib get pap
dem lick him pan him hed
but it tuff like led
dem kick him in him seed
an it started to bleed.

Mama,
Ah jus coudn stan-up deh
an noh dhu notn:

soh mi jook one in him eye
an him started to cry;
mi tump one in him mout
an him started to shout
mi kick one pan him shin
an him started to spin
mi tump him pan him chin
an him drap pan a bin

an crash
an ded.

Mama,
more policeman come dung
an beat mi to di grung;
dem charge Jim fi sus,
dem charge mi fi murdah.

Mama,
dont fret,
dont get depres
an doun-hearted.
Be af good courage
till I hear fram you.

I remain,
your son,
Sonny.

*Sus: short for suspicion, the Vagrancy Act, a piece of 19th century legislation used by racist police officers to criminalize young blacks throughout the 1970s.

The Red Lights of Plenty

Tony Harrison

*for the centenary of the death of Karl Marx,
died London, 14 March 1883*

'... *et asperi
Martis sanguineas quae cohibet manus,
quae dat belligeris foedera gentibus
et cornu retinet divite copiam.*'
(*Seneca,* Medea 62-65)

Though aging and abused still half benign
this petrified PLENTY spilling from her horn
the Old World's edibles, the redskins' corn,
next to the Law Court's Fallout Shelter sign
the blacks and oranges of Hallowe'en.
All that motherly bounty turned to stone!
She chokes back tears of dribbling gasoline
for the future fates of countries like my own.

I stroll round Washington. November strews
red welcomes on the pavements from the trees
on Constitution and Independence Avenues
as if the least pedestrians were VIPs
or returning warlords lured inside to hack,
their lifeblood gushing out this hue of Fall
bulldozed by Buick and by Cadillac
to side drains too choked up to take it all.

Through two museums, *Science* and *Indian Arts*
something from deep below the car-choked street,
like thousands of Poe's buried tell-tale hearts
pounds with a bass and undissembled beat.
With NASA decals, necklaces by Navajo,
Japanese in groups come out to stare
at the demolition that they'd felt below
their feet, choking this chill Sunday air.

The American Wrecking Co.'s
repeatedly rammed iron wrecking ball
swinging in arcs of rhythmic tos and fros
against a scarcely-50-year-old, well-built wall
cracks cement from criss-cross steel supports,
and, floor by floor, once guaranteed to last
till time needs more museums, Justice Courts,
and enterprises space, collapses to the past.

A red light flashes many times a minute
on the Population Clock here in D.C.
to show the billions the World has in it
including those police, that black youth, me,
and, three years ago today, reached 4.5!
Each line of verse how many people born?
How many of these children will survive
crushed through the narrow end of PLENTY's horn?

And one red light for punished and for pitied
the FBI displays next to the time
flashes on whenever there's committed
somewhere in the States a serious crime,
as I imagine that it flashed on when the youth
I see handcuffed and then screeched away
to monuments of Justice, Order, Truth,
committed his, but what it was I couldn't say.

An All Souls' pumpkin rots on someone's porch.
It could be PLENTY's head, about to die,
her cornucopia a guttering torch
still hot enough to scorch the whole Earth dry.
This pumpkin lantern's gouged eyes glued
against some unbelievably bright glare
can't see, as I do, that young black pursued
then caught, the red lights hacking darkening air.

Leaves, some like menses, some volcanic hues,
whirl on successive wafts of hot CO
as Constitution and Independence Avenues
boom to the ball and chain's destructive blow
and, against Virginia, on Capital and Law
each sunset-reddened window one degree
of vast thermometers that, floor by floor,
chart our fever up to World War Three.

In a poem this long how many new souls born?
How many pendulum swings of wreckers' ball
that throbs beneath the White House on whose lawn
a giant vacuum's Hoovering the Fall?

Fighters For Life

Michael Rosen

Our mothers and fathers
fought the thugs who came to torment them in the streets
They organised in their places of work
against magnates
who were pouring milk down mines
starving out miners
building bombers
and hobnobbing with Hitler

They fought the Nazi Axis
with the planes and tanks and machines of destruction

and millions wept.

Such a tale of separation of lovers
of brothers, of sisters, of children
of husbands, fathers or mothers
such a fall of streets, towns, countries
and continents had never been known.

So much — so quickly
so much killing, plunder and ruin
so much energy, so much power
so many brains, so many hands
making machines to break machines.

Out of the blood and oil
out of the iron and steel
out of the fires and infernos
the burnt wastelands, the pits and heaps of broken bones
our mothers and fathers came together
and with them came the oil-owners
iron-owners, steel-owners
fire-owners, inferno-makers,
waste-makers, home-breakers.

They weren't in the sewers of Warsaw
they weren't on Main Street, Hiroshima
they weren't eating rats in Leningrad
they didn't queue in the markets or at Auschwitz
they didn't set light to their own roofs
to stop enemies sheltering under them
they didn't stand at the benches and lathes
beg for water, wash pants, boil a potato, or pick apples.
They didn't even lift the gold they hoarded.

This gang of dictators, commanders,
chiefs and bossmen
discuss how the power that lies
in the earth of the Earth shall be shared
and commandeer the men, women and children
on the earth of the Earth to get it.

There is no trail of destruction of living things,
no trick, no system, no pain
no breaking of bodies
no sickness, paralysis or torment
no hunger, fear, fever or cold
that these men will ever hold back
from leaving in their path

Who dies for them?
who dies in Haiphong harbour
or on the streets of Derry.
who dies in the football stadium of Santiago
who dies for Rio-Tinto Zinc
and the grand Consolidated Gold Mine

who gets maimed
making, building, washing,
digging and cleaning?
Who falls, who drops before their time?

People who have nothing
people who start every day
with nothing but their heads and bodies
people who hope to have strength enough
to work enough
to get food enough
to build up their strength enough
to work enough

fighters for life

Against this force of world work
a cellarful of worldwide chiefs and operators
rule and penetrate
every street corner, vineyard, barrack and mine
the fish-nets, stables and broom-cupboards,
the beaches, hospital bays and stoves.

Fighters for life
makers of life
lovers of life
now we need ways of coming together
and holding together
where we fight for life
where we make and love that life
or we will be called up for the armies of destruction
for the cellarful of worldwide operators
and so live to die.

Balthazar's Poem

Chris Searle

I was born a white boy
        in a white boy's world.
I never met a black man
        except Man Friday
        and whispers of the Mau-Mau.
When I was ten in the London suburbs
they covered me with black boot polish
all over arms, face, legs
        put a crown on my head
and I was the King of Ethiopia,
Balthazar they called me
        bringing myrrh to Jesus —
whatever that was, they never told me.
It took a month to rub the blackness off
and I was chapped and red and raw like pigmeat.

The first black man I ever met
was a man called Wesley Hall.
I was thirteen
        he was an unknown sportsman
on his first tour of my country.
I asked for his autograph at Ilford Cricket Ground
as he stood, shy and huge
        smiled, and wrote for me.
I loved him.

Then his friend Gilchrist came whirling
pounding, stamping, hurling
he bowled bullets at my countrymen.
This was sport, but something else too.
He moved with a fury
        an anger like a storm
like the Mau-Mau he was a soldier
like the men in Malaya he was a guerrilla

217

like the warriors in Cyprus he was a hero
a new world was rising in the tornado of his arms
the trajectory of his hurling was at the heart of all things
    evil.

Then a man named Collie Smith
                swung his bat like a sword
he had a sword in his hand
and something new was sweeping England's turf
something heavier was rolling the ground
and cutting from the past.
When Wes bowled
            magnificence was born for me
I never knew it before
I tried, I strove, I imitated
I found my own way,
            my own action
and every time I hurled
            I sought to touch his power.

Now I have lived in black lands of freedom
made common ground by systems of love,
the mist of history is clearing
and Balthazar's polish seems to take a new hue
and ground from the skin
            deep into my flesh and bone
the truth is forever growing —
Gilchrist's Caribbean is our common ground
The mountains of Ethiopia are our common ground:
Ilford Cricket Ground is our common ground
The earth of tomorrow is our common ground.

Remembering the invasion of Grenada by the USA*

Bob Dixon

Long ago, I burnt all those books:
Marx, Engels, Lenin
and, of course, Tony Benn and Michael Foot
— and I couldn't feel safe with Harold Wilson's work
    in the house.

I've got rid of my tools:
the hammers, chisels, the saw and the axe
— anything that might be used as a weapon.
I don't think the garage could be put to any military use
but I'm knocking it down anyway.
You can't be too careful.

There isn't a Cuban anywhere in the house
and I wouldn't have any US citizens here.
They might have to be rescued.
And I've put the cat out
to be on the safe side.
I'm sure she has a bit of Persian in her.

Anyway, I don't think I'm a threat to the United States
    now.
Do you think they'll still invade?

*and remembering, also, the US annexation of Hawaii and Puerto Rico and the US military intervention in: Afghanistan, Albania, Bolivia, Cambodia, Chad, China, Colombia, the Congo, Costa Rica, Cuba, the Dominican Republic, El Salvador, Greece, Guatemala, Haiti, Honduras, Indonesia, Iraq, Korea, Laos, Lebanon, Libya, Mexico, Nicaragua, Panama, Peru, the Philippines, Somalia, South Yemen, Soviet Russia, the Sudan, Thailand, Venezuela, Vietnam and Yugoslavia. (This list may be incomplete.) Also, remembering US interference, of various other kinds, in these and most other countries, most of the time.

Cuba, Crocodiles, Rain

Keith Armstrong

It is raining on Crocodiles,
bullet-tears on the scales.
Here, where the balance of power has changed.
These banks of hardened green-backs, spread
stoned along the water's edge,
are caged
like old dictators,
reigns ended
as young Cuba
surrounds them.

Waterpot

Grace Nichols

The daily going out
and coming in
always being hurried
along
like like... cattle

In the evenings
returning from the fields
she tried hard to walk
like a woman

she tried very hard
pulling herself erect
with every three or four
steps
pulling herself together
holding herself like
royal cane

And the overseer
hurrying them along
in the quickening darkness

And the overseer sneering
them along in the quickening
darkness

sneered at the pathetic —
the pathetic display
of dignity

O but look
there's a waterpot growing
from her head

Red Rebel Song

Jean Binta Breeze

is lang time
i waan sing dis song
    sing it loud
    sing it long
    no apology
    no pun
jus a raw fire madness
a clinging to de green
a sargasso sea

is years
of ungluing Iself
from de fabric of lust
dat have I
in a pin-up glare

years
of trying to buil
de trust

lang time I waan
free Iself
from de white black question
from de constant hairpulling
breadfruit baiting
coconut shaking
hypocrisies
    of I skin
    having nutten to do
but lie dung
pon Massa bed
outside

an certain bway
weh ah entertain
delegation after delegation
an still kyan solve
a likkle irrigation
shoulda jus get lick
an stamp pon a envelope
wid no return address

    nuff sista an bredda like I
red wid anger
kyan explode
    is I an I leg split
    open
cross dis sea
of hatred an indifference
    tekkin injection after injection
fi cure di madness an pull we foot togedda
    is I an I
did climb mountain
an try carry a cloudful
a tears
pon we head
so Noah wouln't haffi
buil a nex ark
fi save we fram de waters

    I is de red rebel
woman
    holding eart
north pole to
south
    tropical
    wet
heating whole continents wid a
    rain forest intensity
let go eida side
    is to lose part of I

                bridge
                over troubled water lay
        some loving on I now
                watch I
                painted halfbreed
                centrespread
                I nah
                tek no abuse fram eida direction
                I is
        red ribba
        foot shape outa country clay
                Madda
        of white children red children an black
                who!

        lang time
        I waan sing dis song
                sing it loud
                sing it long
                no apology
                no pun
        jus a rawfire madness
        a clinging to de green
        a sargasso sea

                I release Iself
                from de promise
                of eternal compromise
                from de bed of rapists
                black or white
                from page 3
                from

                cho
                if I waan gi yuh piece
                is mine
                free
                no apology

lang time I reaping
byblows
peepshows
whoknows
wat amount of dose

I live it
I feel it
I sing it

it don't mek life no easier
but it sure don't mek it wrong

I is de free christian
who know Jah
de one who roam
an come home
I is de red rebel
woman
accepting I madness
declaring I song
nah siddung eena attic
tek no fire bun
I singing it loud
I singing it long
think seh I done
well
I jus a come
    I I I own rainbow
    I I I own song

Mother... Sister... Daughter...

Jean Binta Breeze

'If you should see me,
walking down the street,
mouth muffled
head low against the wind,
know
that this is no woman bent
on sacrifice
just
heavy
with the thoughts
of freedom...'

The Queen of Sheba

Kathleen Jamie

Scotland, you have invoked her name
just once too often
in your Presbyterian living rooms.
She's heard, yea
even unto heathenish Arabia
your vixen's bark of poverty, come down
the family like a lang neb, a thrawn streak,
a wally dug you never liked
but can't get shot of.

She's had enough. She's come.
Whit, tae this dump? Yes!
She rides first camel
of a swaying caravan
from her desert sands
to the peat and bracken
of the Pentland hills
across the fit-ba pitch
to the thin mirage
of the swings and chute; scattered with glass.

Breathe that steamy musk
on the Curriehill Road, not mutton-shanks
boiled for broth, nor the chlorine stink
of the swimming pool where skinny girls
accuse each other of verrucas.
In her bathhouses women bear
warm pot-bellied terracotta pitchers
on their laughing hips.
All that she desires, whatever she asks
She will make the bottled dreams
of your wee lasses
look like *sweeties*.

Spangles scarcely cover
her gorgeous breasts, hanging gardens
jewels, frankincense; more voluptuous
even than Vi-next-door, whose
high-heeled slippers
keeked from dressing gowns
like little hooves, wee tails
of pink fur stuffed in the cleavage of her toes;
more audacious even than Currie Liz
who led the gala floats
through the Wimpey scheme
in a ruby-red Lotus Elan
before the Boys' Brigade band
and the Brownies' borrowed coal-truck;
hair piled like candy-floss;
who lifted her hands from the neat wheel
to tinkle her fingers
at her tricks
    among the Masons and the elders and the police.

The cool black skin
of the Bible couldn't hold her,
nor the atlas green
on the kitchen table,
you stuck with thumbs
and split to fruity hemispheres —
yellow Yemen, Red Sea, *Ethiopia*. Stick in
with the homework and you'll be
cliver like yer faither,
but no too cliver,
no *above yersel*.

See her lead those great soft camels
widdershins round the kirk-yaird,
smiling
as she eats
avocados with apostle spoons
she'll teach us how. But first

she wants to strip the willow
she desires the keys
    to the National Library
she is beckoning
    the lasses
    in the awestruck crowd...
Yes, we'd like to
    clap the camels,
to smell the spice,
admire her hairy legs and
bonny wicked smile, we want to take
PhDs in Persian, be vice
to her president: we want
to help her
    ask some Difficult Questions

she's shouting for our wisest man
to test her mettle:

    Scour Scotland for a Solomon!

Sure enough: from the back of the crowd
someone growls:
    whae do you think y'ur?

and a thousand laughing girls and she
draw our hot breath
    and shout:

THE QUEEN OF SHEBA!

It Has Happened

Jack Lindsay

It has happened all before, and yet
it has all to happen. So it seems.
Darker grows the maniac threat
and richer swell the answering dreams.
Just past our straining fingertips
it lies. And that's the very thing
they said two thousand years ago,
broken, with hope unslackening.
At every gain, away it slips.
In struggle, entire and strong it grows;
the bonds of brotherhood hold fast.
Someday the treacherous gap will close
and we'll possess the earth at last.

Interference Song

Liz Lochhead

It's TV Newstime —
It's us and them.
Our brave police passively resist
the undemocratic NUM.
Let's wave the flagging Falklands
that was a TV War —
But the screen goes blank
on El Salvador.

It's a TV election
Labour would knock 'em cold
if there weren't something wrong
with the horizontal hold.
The SDP Alliance
is decidedly lukewarm,
and Thatcher talks platitudes
in a snowstorm.

There is some interference
but this is what you get
Do not adjust your attitudes
Do not adjust your set —
The Great British public
is all too bossable —
Normal service will be resumed
as soon as possible.

If it's TV for kids
then you're *white* we presume
and watching with mother
in a Surrey living room?
If it's TV ads
"The Best Thing on the Box"
you can get all these goodies
if you pull up your socks.

It it's TV for women
it's strictly soft soap
and afternoon crochet —
how to cook, how to cope.
If it's TV for men
then it's something to do
with a bat or a ball
or a billiard cue.

There is some interference
but this is what you get
Do not adjust your attitudes
Do not adjust your set —
The Great British public
is all too bossable
Normal service will be resumed
as soon as possible.

It's a TV minority
being given its fair say
Black is beautiful!
I'm Glad to Be Gay!
For Asians in Britain.
The Gaelic News —
If you watch after midnight
you might just hear our views.

It's TV nostalgia
Where Are They Now?
Lord Reith in his dinner suit,
Lady Barnett take a bow.
Cut glass ex-cents
'cause they'd standards to set.
Newsreels of the thirties
lest we forget.

There is some interference
but this is what you get,
Do not adjust your attitudes
Do not adjust your set
If the Great British Public
is really this bossable,
Normal service will be resumed
as soon as possible.

Telling Myself

Kay Ekevall

I leapt out of bed as if stung
By the chill of Greenham Common,
Cold steel of the Juntas,
Blue gun-barrels in the backs of African miners.

I, lying idly, putting off typing
The Minutes of the last Peace meeting.

Damp cells of prisons penetrated my mind,
The shiver of bullets seeking guerrillas.
Hungry families of Lebanon camps
Icy fear stalking the streets of Belfast.

I, sitting, warm-clad, writing a poem
To the enduring on the barricades.

Promises

Liz Lochhead

Puffed up promises
On TV ads
Make you want what you never had

All you Persil Mums
And Flora Dads
Say you live just for the Kids

All you want is for things to be right!
Its Comfort Soft
Its Whiter than white

Buy them Heinz's Beans
Never forget
To buy the fruitgums for Mum's pet

Puffed up promises
Puffed up wheat
Safety. Warmth. Enough to Eat

All you want
Is Life for them all
But who'll be to blame
If the bombs start to fall?

So count the cost of the holocaust
Stand up and fight
For peace.

Good Sunday

John Lucas

This is the day when, under beneficent skies,
citizens wander free and at their ease,
or paired at café-tables make their eyes

do the tongue's daring work, say "love me, please"
and know a kind reply for once is meant.
Here, in a sun-filled park, sweet-scented trees

sprinkle their balm on all who circumvent,
while this day lasts, strict laws of time and place,
who in the candid, fertile air invent

fresh worlds of amity that turn to grace
abounding fears: of cancer, work, the bomb —
those high-banked fears gathering over days

in which we try to make ourselves at home.
But who can bear to live without the light?
Who's acold now? Why, every poor Tom,

Dick and Harry. Then kiss the world good night
or sing for love of warmth and take as theme
such breezy words as put dark clouds to flight.

Not without hope we suffer and we dream

History Teacher in the Warsaw Ghetto Rising
after an engraving by Maurice Mendjisky

Evangeline Paterson

The schoolmaster once known as
Umbrella Feet
unfolds his six-foot length
of gangling bone

and, mild as usual,
blinks — his bi-focals
having gone the way of his pipe
and his tree-shaded study
and his wife Charlotte —

and, jacket flapping, as usual,
carpet slippers treading
rubble of smashed cellars,

advancing steadily into the
glare of the burning street

and holding his rifle uncertainly
as if he thought it irrelevant
— as indeed it is —

he leads his scattered handful
of scarecrow twelve-year-olds

towards the last few minutes
of their own brief history.

Thirty Years On

Charles Hobday

Keeping my head above the millions
who neither know nor care a damn about me
any more than I do about them
I find London the loneliest place in the world.
Yet there I've reforged broken links, researched
into my prehistory, discovered friends
of thirty years ago masquerading
as schoolmasters, trade union presidents
and mothers of three grownup sons.

As I relax my stiffened mind
in a warm bath of nostalgia
I try to reconcile the men I knew
with what they've now become.
Glyn's teaching up in Norfolk. Roy's in airports
and wades through fivers to the bathroom.
When last heard of Philip was in Tass,
Johnnie a wing commander. Norman's knighted
(I wonder if he's kept his party card).
Bill died of t.b. twenty years ago
and Alan in a tank in Normandy.
We know what we are (or do we?)
but don't know what we may be.

The familiar names evoke
evenings in Cambridge rooms
of beer and bawdy songs and endless talk
on poetry, God, sex and revolution,
uneasily assumed sophistication
masking the guilty secret we were virgins.
Our ears were deafened with the crash
of falling Babylon and we were happy
to know ourselves the generation destined
to build the Holy City on its ruins.

Babylon's still doing nicely, thank you,
and every one of us has made
his private compromise except
Alan, lucky man, who died
for something he could still believe in.
The rest of us go wrapped in
what tatters of integrity are left us,
sometimes remembering with a guilty smile
the days when innocence came easily.

My Study

E.P. Thompson

King of my freedom here, with every prop
A poet needs — the small hours of the night,
A harvest moon above an English copse...

Backward unrationalised trade, its furthest yet
Technology this typewriter which goes
With flailing arms through the ripe alphabet.

Not even bread the pen is mightier than.
Each in its statutory place the giants yawn:
I blow my mind against their sails and fan

The mills that grind my own necessity.
Oh, royal me! Unpoliced imperial man
And monarch of my incapacity

To aid my helpless comrades as they fall
Lumumba, Nagy, Allende: alphabet
Apt to our age! In answer to your call

I rush out in this rattling harvester
And thrash you into type. But what I write
Brings down no armoured bans, no Ministers

Of the Interior interrogate.
None bothers to break in and seize
My verses for subversion of the state:

Even the little dogmas do not bark.
I leave my desk and peer into the world.
Outside the owls are hunting. Dark

Has harvested the moon. Imperial eyes
Quarter the ground for fellow creaturehood:
Small as the hour some hunted terror cries.

I go back to my desk. If it could fight
Or dream or mate, what other creature would
Sit making marks on paper through the night?

September, 1973

Ghost Stations

Carole Satyamurti

We are the inheritors. We hide here
at the roots of the perverted city
waiting, practising the Pure Way.
Listening to ourselves, each other,
we find the old soiled words won't do;
often we can only dance our meanings.

Deep in the arteries of London, life
is possible — in the forgotten stations:
York Road, St Mary's, Seething Lane...
I love the names. Each day, we sing them
like a psalm, a celebration
— Down Street, British Museum, City Road.

We live on waste. After the current's off
we run along tunnels, through sleeping trains,
ahead of the night cleaners. We find chips,
apple cores (the most nutritious part),
dregs of Coke. On good days, we pick up
coins that fit the chocolate machines.

Once I found a whole bag of shopping.
That night we had an iceberg lettuce,
a honeydew melon, tasting of laughter.
And once, an abutilon — its orange
bee-flowers gladdened us for weeks.
Such things are dangerous;

then, to remind ourselves, we read
the newspapers we use as mattresses.
Or gather on the platforms,
witness the trains as they rip past
(our eyes have grown used to the speed).
Almost every known depravity

is acted out on trains — rape, drunkenness,
robbery, fighting, harassment, abuse.
And the subtler forms — intellectual bullying,
contempt, all the varieties of indifference...
We've learned to read the faces;
we need to see these things, simply.

The travellers only see their own reflections.
But lately, a few in such despair
they cup their faces to the glass,
weeping, have seen the ghost stations
and though we're always out of sight,
they sense our difference and find their way.

Our numbers are growing, though there are
reverses. Some lose heart, want to leave.
We can't let them — we keep them all at
Brompton Road, carefully guarded,
plotting uselessly, swapping fantasies,
raving of sunlight, mountains or the sea.

One day, we'll climb out, convert the city!
The trains are full of terrible energy;
we only have example, words. But there is
our chant to strengthen us, our hope-names:
Uxbridge Road, King William Street,
South Kentish Town, South Acton, Bull and Bush...

Sleeper

Ken Worpole

He would travel
Disguised as an Englishman

A succession of jobs, study, then marriage
He moved to a safe house in the city

Climbed the ladder steadily
Took a different route to work each day

Cultivated friends
Established a network of contacts

Over the years he learnt
To love the native countryside

The rolling downs, the ox-bow valleys,
Dry stone walls and Norman churches

Learnt to swim in cold dark rivers
Bathe in the rusty, groaning sea

No one would guess
That behind drawn curtains, late at night

He would sift through files
Pore over government reports

Make long phone calls to other cities
Set up meetings, plan demonstrations

Type out notes from informal conversations
Study the works of murdered intellectuals

Write poems in code
Keep a diary of metaphors

Send letters abroad
Which he posted last thing at night

In the letter box by the park gates
Listening to the wind in the chestnut trees

Looking up at the stars and the moon
Half hidden by clouds

The dreams of insurrection fading
More worried about the roses in the garden

Waiting for further orders
The call to action, which never came.

1984

Such Small
Victories

if keir hardie was the man on the moon

Paul Summers

what would he make of it? we wondered;
looking down, night after serious night,
on the ancient tiles of our street:
just hanging there in the indigo
like a stringless conker,
distant & ownerless &
fingering the cello curve
of his immaculate tash.
he'd be stunned by our quiet world,
perplexed at our lack of shift patterns,
our weekend hangovers. our luxurious carpets,
& he'd notice the chimneys no longer smoked.
he'd see our fitted wardrobes bulge
with fake armani, in tasteful
soft pastels & unbleached linen.
he'd study our satellite dishes,
watch open university programmes
in the dead of night, learn envy
from the billboard ads,
grow hungry for the horsepower
of our nippy five-door peugeots.
just before morning, he'd shift his gaze,
browse the horizons in search of old haunts;
he'd wake up the tramp on the library steps,
inquire on the whereabouts of some lost friend,
& then he'd remember he's the man on the moon
& not know whether to laugh or cry.

Baz and the Freedom of the Press

Kevin Cadwallender

Full of Hell,
Baz gatecrashes the chip-shop,
bringing down on the counter a greasy
newspaper, bearing a colour image
of a topless model.

"It's a fucking disgrace, you should
watch what you're selling,
I bought them chips for my little girl"

The chip-shop owner
is caught somewhere between
bemused and terrified and
pours two lots of vinegar
on some wifie's tail-end.

He stutters meekly,
"But.. but.. I only sell chips!"

Baz rumbles on about guards in Auschwitz
and then explodes,
"Bloody typical, I bet you're a Tory,
Only a bloody Tory rag
would print this filth
and only a Tory would
wrap up my little girl's chips
in pornography.

"But... But..."

The chip-shop queue
are nodding their agreement
and checking their wrappings
for nudes.

The poor bastard is sweating now
and apologising, he offers Baz
a free Fish and Chip lunch.
Baz graciously accepts the offer.
The queue warmly applauds his exit.

Outside I remind Baz
that he hasn't got a little girl
and he reminds me
who's got the free lunch.

The Restricting Gate

Alan Dent

I'm watching the news and the workers
At Jaguar, Coventry, have voted
For a series of one-day strikes.
The commentator
Stands outside the factory while
Behind him and to left and right
The men rush out of the gate
On foot, by car and also
A solitary cyclist, young
Changing gear on his racer.
I see them, his kind, every day
A herd of riders at five
And I always wonder what
They fly towards so eagerly:
Wives and girlfriends?
Children?
Mother's tea early on the table?
Beer, football, pigeons, darts
Gardens? Or merely to flop
Before the television, sleepy
Forgetting the last eight line-hours
Not thinking about the next.
That cyclist, I like him
In all his versions
Small, vulnerable, human against
The factory huge and man-devouring.
I wish him a happy strike
A lie-in with his wife
Or girlfriend
A day of laziness and freedom
Or a busy day doing
The things the factory keeps him from.
I wish him sunshine and
I wish his strike days might seem

Like the shape of a new world
The factory in his mind shrinking, the man
Growing, changing gear on his racer, leaving
The restricting gate
For the last time.

HMS Glasshouse

Sean O'Brien

At this hour the park offers only
A steam-heated acre of glass,
A sign in fresh hardboard, and somewhere
To wait while appearing to act.

We step inside its vaulted heat,
Its bleared below-decks light. We taste
Its air of rot and counter-rot, attend
Its vegetable politics, and watch

As plants with webbed and shellacked hands
Swarm up the stanchions, offering
The universal shrug of making do,
Like the teenagers painting the catwalks,

Who might once have painted the hulls
Of the frigates and merchantmen sent
To secure the Malvinas for mutton.
Their status as national assets has lapsed

And the registers cancel their names:
They are guilty again, as am I, as are you,
As the glasshouse sweats on
Like the *Unterseeboot* of the State

With its periscope down, its orders sealed,
Its routine a deliberate torpor.
We wake in the very same place
With the curious notion that fish

Have been crowding the glass to peer in
At the items preserved for the voyage —
Cast-iron and Pilkingtons' finest,
Odd volumes of Oakeshott and Scruton

To kill off the time, in an atmosphere
Soon to be poison. Let's make our inspection
On tiptoe, and listen for cracks
In case one of us throws the first stone.

In Conference

Gordon Hodgeon

I am looking out, the window
to a wider understanding
beyond all this paper talk
on the fifth floor of *The Imperial*
and there is clear evidence that
these Harrogate chimney pots
are in charge, manage the great sky
and its unknowing hosts,
their swell and their migration.

Though it is done without a flicker,
laid down with the stones,
without questioning of destiny,
a century of smokefall
dark on the parapets up here
for us all to admire,
at the top, in the *Empire Suite*,
the unchanging arrogance
of crowns on high-set heads.

If the sun screams of fire or the clouds
shake in revolutionary dance,
these chimney pots are in charge, they manage
the great sky, at whose eye-rim
a green tide lifts. Hills, woods and dales.

There we learn to swim, begin in that flesh
to speak the language of the deep,
welcome its overwhelm, the toppling at last
of chimney pots, this Harrogate regime.

Comprehensive

Carol Ann Duffy

Tutumantu is like hopscotch, Kwani-kwani is like
    hide-and-seek.
When my sister came back to Africa she could only speak
English. Sometimes we fought in bed because she didn't
    know
what I was saying. I like Africa better than England.
My mother says You will like it when we get our own
    house.
We talk a lot about the things we used to do
in Africa and then we are happy.

Wayne. Fourteen. Games are for kids. I support
the National Front. Paki-bashing and pulling girls'
knickers down. Dad's got his own mini-cab. We watch
the video. I Spit on Your Grave. Brilliant.
I don't suppose I'll get a job. It's all them
coming over here to work. Arsenal.

Masjid at 6 o'clock. School at 8. There was
a friendly shop selling rice. They ground it at home
to make the evening nan. Families face Mecca.
There was much more room to play than here in London.
We played in an old village. It is empty now.

Making Money

Carol Ann Duffy

Turnover. Profit. Readies. Cash. Loot. Dough. Income.
    Stash.
Dosh. Bread. Finance. Brass. I give my tongue over
to money; the taste of warm rust in a chipped mug
of tap-water. Drink some yourself. Consider
an Indian man in Delhi, Salaamat the *niyariwallah*,
who squats by an open drain for hours, sifting shit
for the price of a chapati. More than that. His hands
in crumbling gloves of crap pray at the drains
for the pearls in slime his grandfather swore he found.

Megabucks. Wages. Interest. Wealth. I sniff and snuffle
for a whiff of pelf; the stench of an abattoir blown
by a stale wind over the fields. Roll up a fiver,
snort. Meet Kim. Kim will give you the works,
her own worst enema, suck you, lick you, squeal
red weals to your whip, be nun, nurse, nanny,
nymph on a credit card. Don't worry.
Kim's only in it for the money. Lucre. Tin. Dibs.

I put my ear to brass lips; a small fire's whisper
close to a forest. Listen. His cellular telephone
rings in the Bull's car. Golden hello. Big deal. Now get this
straight. *Making a living is making a killing these days.*
Jobbers and brokers buzz. He paints out a landscape
by number. The Bull. Seriously rich. Nasty. One of us.

Salary. Boodle. Oof. Blunt. Shekels. Lolly. Gelt. Funds.
I wallow in coin, naked; the scary caress of a fake hand
on my flesh. Get stuck in. Bergama. The boys from the
    bazaar
hide on the target-range, watching the soldiers fire.
    Between bursts,
they rush for the spent shells, cart them away for scrap.

Here is the catch. Some shells don't explode. Ahmat
runs over grass, lucky for six months, so far. So
bomb-collectors die young. But the money's good.

Palmgrease. Smackers. Greenbacks. Wads. I widen my eyes
at a fortune; a set of knives on black cloth, shining,
utterly beautiful. Weep. The economy booms
like cannon, far out at sea on a lone ship. We leave
our places of work, tired, in the shortening hours, in the time
of night our town could be anywhere, and some of us pause
in the square, where a clown makes money swallowing fire.

De Rich Getting Rich

Benjamin Zephaniah

Big Boy Rich wants to mek a profit,
Sue wants a kidney,
Tony wants a job,
Errol wants freedom,
Tom wants clean air to breath.
Rich wants to buy a rocket,
Jenny and Paul want a zebra-crossing,
Ms Campbell de teacher wants recognition,
Old-timer Larry wants a pension
And Sgt. Mollins wants a conviction.
Rich wants old champagne.
Dis child needs fresh water,
Danny needs a pair of shoes,
Mom needs a fifty pence piece for de meter,
And dis guy said if him don't get some kinda
Voice in parliament him will blow de place
Up, and watch it fall down.

Big Boy Rich wants a war.
Him sey him wants to protect Sue, Tony, Errol, Tom,
Jenny, Paul, Ms Campbell, Larry, Sgt Mollins, dis child,
Danny and Mom and many other guys including you and
    me.

Big Boy Rich says he never got where he
Is today by sitting pon his backside
Complaining about the state of de world.

A Proud Shore For Legends

Nicki Jackowska

Well here we are again jumping up and down
upon the shore, eyes all at sea, gobbling
the sand this time (forgetting Malvinas)
dreaming of desert rats, Arabian nights
and all that head-gear. What a year
it's been for camels swaying through our
narrowest needle's-eye. See how our fingers
poke into every pie (greedy before the storm)
into the crack and lull of a sheltering sky,
an inflammation of the digit and the tongue.
And see how the little bastard inside us all
waves his tomahawk, his tommy and his rattle
for our team didn't they, haven't they always won?

The boy with a mission polishes his gun
watching planes soar like silk-moths
into that deepening black of where he's
banished cat's-paw touch and raspberry-cane.
For he's American and they have smooth-talked
him and tidied up his plot to put him straight.
All he can do is wait on the shore of sand
securely tarnished. And in his right hand
(silky on the gun) a lifeline leaps and jerks
across the palm then stops before the cleft,
dirt-riddled gulf between his finger and his thumb.

They don't tell, don't let on. The screens
of Europe and the USA have made him legend.
At nineteen he's the son of light, a mine
of interference; fuzzy lines upon a grid.
And soon the great lid of the desert-eye
will blink just once and out damned spot he'll go
lancing the wound that never can be bled.
Just like Miss Havisham's wedding captured

in a cobweb before the consummation. No, boy
they'll never marry nor stamp each other out.
But you'll be gone before you know it, and so
the story won't be told you see, the legend.

After Eighteen Years of This Sort of Thing

Mark Robinson

I will put my best heart forward and hope
for a dip in the attentions of the day.
The rational city plays a peeping game
behind the headlines and the U-turns,
our friends' necessary betrayals.

The reversals, the blockage, the lost
and irreplaceable gather at our gate,
like snails that crunch under the children's feet.
The afternoon feels like an in-joke
no one can fully explain. I'm so tired

of being English in this shabby excuse
for what might be, so thoroughly tired
of feeling like a man questioning the rules
of cricket or football — why *can't* he touch it
with his hand? —I can hardly breath these words.

But if I've inherited one thing from
my family it's a stubborn streak as wide
as the Ribble. I am going to sit here until
the image of Portillo at the stake
disappears from my morbid mind.

And then tomorrow you and I will take the kids
to the allotment, where we will plant sunflowers
on our communal land to mark the beginning
of the end. To such small victories am I reduced.
The light fades suddenly, is swallowed by evening.

A Ballad for Apothecaries

Anne Stevenson

In sixteen-hundred-and-sixteen
(The year Will Shakespeare died),
Earth made a pact with a curious star,
And a newborn baby cried.

Queen Bess's bright spring was over,
James Stuart frowned from the throne;
A more turbulent, seditious people
England had never known.

Now, Nick was a winsome baby,
And Nick was a lively lad,
So they gowned him and sent him to Cambridge
Where he went, said the priests, to the bad.

For though he excelled in Latin
And could rattle the Gospels in Greek,
He thought to himself, there's more to be said
Than the ancients knew how to speak.

He was led to alchemical studies
Through a deep Paracelsian text.
He took up the art of astrology first,
And the science of botany next.

To the theories of Galen he listened,
And to those of Hippocrates, too,
But he said to himself, there's more to be done
Than the ancients knew how to do.

For though Dr Tradition's a rich man,
He charges a rich man's fee.
Dr Reason and Dr Experience
Are my guides in philosophy.

The College of Learned Physicians
Prescribes for the ruling class:
Physick for the ills of the great, they sneer,
Won't do for the vulgar mass.

But I say the heart of a beggar
Is as true as the heart of a king,
And the English blood in our English veins
Is of equal valuing.

Poor Nick fell in love with an heiress,
But en route to their desperate tryst,
The lady was struck down by lightning
Before they'd embrased or kissed.

So our hero consulted the Heavens
Where he saw he was fated to be
A friend to the sick and the humble
But the Great World's enemy.

Nick packed up his books in Cambridge
And came down without a degree
To inspirit Red Lion Street, Spitalfields,
With his fiery humanity.

As a reckless, unlicensed physician,
He was moved to disseminate
Cures for the ills of the body
With cures for the ills of the state.

Who knows what horrors would have happened
To Nicholas Culpeper, Gent.,
If the king hadn't driven his kingdom
Into war with Parliament.

In the ranks of the New Model Army
Nick fought with the medical men,
Till a Royalist bullet at Newbury
Shot him back to his thundering pen.

'Scholars are the people's jailors,
And Latin's their jail,' he roared,
'Our fates are in thrall to knowledge;
Vile men would have knowledge obscured!'

When they toppled King Charles's head off
Nick Culpeper cried, 'Amen!'
It's well that he died before the day
They stuck it on again.

Still, English tongues won their freedom
In those turbulent years set apart;
And the wise, they cherish Nick's courage
While they cheer his compassionate heart.

So whenever you stop in a chemist's
For an aspirin or salve for a sore,
Give a thought to Nicholas Culpeper
Who dispensed to the London poor.

For cures for the ills of the body
Are cures for the ills of the mind;
And a welfare state is a sick state
When the dumb are led by the blind.

Millet's *The Gleaners*

Matt Simpson

Watch out for the bloke astride the horse —
the blocker-man – keeping measured distances

between himself and us, between us and
the fixed horizon, hedges ending fields;

puissant and upright for now — though vertical's
a better word — with such an arrogance between his legs

there only needs a twitch of rein, a squeeze of thigh
to curb its titillating twitchiness

or spring its energies, velocities on us.
Keep backs to him and keep your distances,

fidget your fingers in the stubble. That's
the language he allows:

consonants, vowels of breaking backs,
sibilance of grain.

About Benwell

Gillian Allnutt

Perhaps there will always be yellow buses
passing and Presto's
and people with faces like broken promises

and shops full of stotties and butties and buckets and
      bubble bath
and bones for broth
where the poor may inherit the earth

and women who will
wade into the wind and waste with hope eternal
and kids like saplings planted by the Council

and William Armstrong's endless line
of bairns, whose names, in sandstone,
rehabilitate their streets of rag and bone

where bits of paper, bottle tops and Pepsi cans blow up
      and down
despondently, like souls on their own.
Perhaps there will always be unremembered men

and maps of Old Dunston and Metroland and the rough
      blown rain
and the riding down of the sun
towards Blaydon.

The Windows of Sarajevo

David Grubb

Here are the smallest windows in the world. Light hovers
but does not enter; it is cold-boned, nervous, an awkward
  signal.
And the child who sits inside this building never bothers
  to look out.
There is nothing. There is no. There is no picture to be
  seen. Instead on
scraps of paper the small girl draws a window that
  becomes a sun,
a rose, a bird of pale blue that flies in making the entire
  room
gold and blue, a whisper of eternity. And even music. It
  is the music
Of skipping ropes, running and bouncing a ball. And
  sometimes
the window lets in smells of food, of flowers. And these
  are extraordinary
butterflies of laughter, and a kite that keeps crossing the
  tree tops,
and the sound of bells. Here are the smallest windows in
  the world
and the child draws what she believes.

Immigrants

Lotte Kramer

The wolves are coming back to Germany.
Across the Polish border
Barricades are down:
The wolves slink into forests in the dark

And bring a darker Russia in their veins.
They sniff out ancient fairy tales
Trading in omens, hunger, fear,
Looking for hidden spaces under rocks.

At night they cluster by the edge of woods
In families of threes and fours,
Howling their wail of loneliness
Over the Eastern villages and plains.

Wolves

Peter Mortimer

You must learn about wolves
One day wolves will circle your fire
While you watch the wolves are unmoving
Your look can freeze them on snow
Look again, the circle is closer
And so the process continues

You cannot always watch them
The more you watch wolves
The more you neglect your fire

You must build your fire hot and high
One day the sky may burn
Let the wolves come in their time
They too are surrounded

The Beasts of England

Andy Croft

The long, long night is o'er at last,
  The beastly tyrant slain,
The light of dawn breaks in the east
  Saluting Freedom's reign!

Though cowards flinch and traitors sneer,
  The last fight's faced and won,
The age of Cant is past at last,
  The age of Truth begun.

For Manor Farm is free again,
  And Farmer Jones restored,
And upstart porkers everywhere
  Have had their bacon cured.

Their nasty brutish, short-lived rule
  Is finally o'erthrown,
And market day in Willingdon
  The drinks are all on Jones.

Arise, arise, and hark ye
  To the news from Manor Farm,
Where beasts are free to roam again
  And England's safe from harm,

Where Nature's just a fable for
  The swinish multitude,
Where some are meant to eat a lot
  But most are meant for food,

Where History can be boiled down
  To just a lump of lard,
And every good idea ends up
  In Alfred Simmond's yard.

But things look bad on Manor Farm,
  And Jones is overdrawn,
The sheep are in the meadow
  And the cows are in the corn,

And the harvest fields are full of weeds,
  And overrun by rats,
And the windmill doesn't work these days
  And the dairy's full of cats,

And in the ruined harvest poppies
  Nod their sleepy heads,
And the sheep and goats are all mixed up,
  And the geese and ducks are dead,

For Jones employs three foxes called
  Dominion, Rank and Greed,
Who guard the hen-house door at night
  For more than chicken-feed.

From Foxwood Farm to Pinchfield Farm
  The masters celebrate
The liberated superpower
  That's now a Third World State,

And toast the Red Lion taproom hero,
  Now turned auctioneer,
Who's selling off his meadows
  Just to keep himself in beer.

And sharp-eyed neighbours shake their heads
  And say it's for the best
It's better to die hungry than
  To eat but be oppressed.

If Manor Farm goes to the dogs
  The reason's plain to see:
The stupid brutes who thought to choose
  To eat but not be free.

So raise the scarlet standard high,
  In every market place,
French fries and coke and burgers shall
  Unite the human race,

Arise ye starvelings, kneel no more,
  Your dreams have come to pass,
You poor and hungry multitudes
  Shall eat your fill of grass.

East of Easter

Neil Astley

For years they came in wonder, filing past
his waxy russet-bearded face. Kazakhs
and Tadjiks saw their colossus, tall as
the Caucasus. Uzbeks and Oyruts gazed
on living legend, the titan who shook

the earth, whose speech made land and landlords quake.
His right hand held the sun, his left a beam
of moonlight flooding the mausoleum.
Awe-struck Ostyaks came from the north to look
at the hunter who'd slain their enemies

on the ice, clubbed the fur-traders like seals,
gave their blood-money and dogs to the poor.
Kirgiz men said Redbeard could overpower
the evil one, drive him beneath the seas
with his magic ring, and knowing no night,

he never slept, withered kulaks with light
from his glowing eyes. He rode a white horse
to lift Armenia's yoke, and stirred up wars
on an eagle's back, putting Whites to flight
from the air; stood atop an armoured car

fist raised at the Finland station, called for
action, with Trotsky now invisible
seen at his side by Petrograd people
welcoming the sealed train, when Commissar
Stalin ran to kiss his turned cheek, a sign

he was his dear disciple (the Georgian
plotting behind his back). When he suffered
heart arrest, he let himself be martyred,
tied with tubes to his deathbed like Aslan,
but breathing into a thousand statues

lifted up his stone-like fist in cities
all over Russia, held out for the day
he'd rise again, when medalled dwarfs would try
to pull him from plinth with ropes and pulleys,
bind him like Gulliver trussed on a truck,

parade him prone through the streets of Simbirsk.
Toy soldiers jerked to life then as he'd proph-
esied, switched off his life support, shut off
the flow of visitors. When the clockwork
generals came to the bed where he'd lain in

state since '24 they found not the man
but a shadow stain like the Turin shroud.
He melted like a wraith into a crowd
of waiting statues moving in a line
like androids, trailing rope and scaffolding.

Vladimir Ilyich in the van, standing
fist raised like an icon, marched his statues
out of Moscow. Where the Volga elbows
the Don, a thousand giants turned, stepping
the steppes like nightwalkers. So Lenin led

his lumbering host out of the promised land,
through the Aral seabed to Samarkand
where Uzbeks joined the horde. On they headed
east of Easter, till he rose: his red beard
caught the light, sun spoke of the dawn ahead.

The Act

William Scammell

Watching all those sexy Czechs
up on the wide, wide screen
with supernatural sound effects
descanting on their lightness of being

as one girl, then another, strips
down to her middle C
while the moving picture slows its steps
round pure anatomy

and Russian tanks roll into Prague
(montage, *fff* on the bass)
and girls like glossy snaps in *Vogue*
don't even think of interruptus

I wonder where the babies are,
who pays the bills, and stuff like that,
which may not rate a heavenly choir
or show-mo-on-the-cello shot

but still the orchestra must eat
between engagements, brush its teeth
if ever they're to consummate
more than the bubble in the bath.

The act, the act! A man invades.
A woman and a country yields.
Middle Europe's torn to shreds.
The lovers kick their lovely heels

up in the sky, and squirm to die
just where the flute runs out of breath,
a nymphs-and-shepherds victory
over the stodgy march of death.

Hold on a bit. There's more to love,
invasion, exile, war and fate
than six bars of Rachmaninov
and humping in a bowler hat

and ideas, in their posy smalls,
chiaroscuro of dark nipples
cutely enamoured of themselves
and questionable parallels.

No tanks came here, yet still and all
the Iron Lady drove to town,
rumbling up against Whitehall,
shooting the concensus down.

Our chief of women, under law,
beseeching everybody's bowels,
who strips state assets from the poor
and has the hots for Samuel Smiles.

She wastes no time on levellers,
Fifth Monarchy men, the liberal wets.
Businessmen and buccaneers
are all she knows of earthly Saints.

While parliament sinks to its knees
and mumbles spells with Tony Benn
the city booms, the placemen squeeze
more blood out of the national stone.

And, like the Czechs, we take to sex
or other fiddles, impotent
as Harold in his Gannex macs
or poor Achilles in his tent.

Age of the TV anchorman,
the rock star, and the page 3 girl.
The fast buck points the way to Zion.

A swelling that you'll never feel
dispenses all the satisfaction
you ain't got, and never will.

Prague meets London; Cracow, Leeds.
Not synonyms, exactly. No!
But take a look at what succeeds
in the art house, next time you go.

Revisionism

Gordon Wardman

"only the best is good enough for the working class"
— Harry Pollitt

— who got off at Edgehill, of course

all we ever seemed to want was more
— jobs, wages, leisure —
socialism was like going to the bookie's
to demand horses that always won

well, Thatcher gave us more (and more)
    loadsamore
fire and water and the houses we lived in
and we lacked the bottle to say
that wasn't what we meant at all

next time, says Tam, I'm gonna
go in with a claymore, wop it
on the counter like King Kong's dong,
less, I'm gonna say, give me less,
you bastards, or it'll be the worse
for you, I'm not kidding, mind,
this is the cultural revolution

A Three Year Ode

W.N. Herbert

I To Gorbachev (1991)
For now in the flower and iron of the truth
To you we turn...
Hugh MacDiarmid
First Hymn to Lenin

Thi cat sits at ma French windies,
irrepressibil, stupit, lyk thi licht
that maun cam in, she moans.

Ut's a cauld dey, thi waurmth oan ma herr,
lyk hir affeckshun, anerly exists
atween thi gless an me. Ootwith

 ut aa blaws loose as meh attenshun
when Eh lat hur in. She waants
aa o me or oot again. Eh sit an feel

licht fill thi hooses in Fife
an the cheek banes o Tay's waves,
Eh rowl wi ut lyk thi cat owre

thi Baltic. Eh'm oan a trenn o licht
speedin fur Moscow, bearin Pasternak
back, shovelt oot o Zhivago's snaa-cell.

 Eh'm oan a trenn o licht speedin
atween thi gless an thi sel,
enterin Russia oan a cat's shouthirs.

Eh'm fu o thi eisenin that wad stoap time
i thi middil o thi page, an force
uts maist donsy passengir

---

maun-must; *anerly*-only; *eisenin*-desire; *donsy*-lovely, vigorous;

oot, tae dance upo thi snaw. Dance,
Liberty, dance! spleet yir sark an
melt aa permafrost wi yir reid wame!

But Liberty nivir fed onywan. An Christ's
poke, tho unca deep, wisna designd
tae clear thi queues, 'Thi puir ur aye wi us.'

Thi licht mairches thru Leningrad streets
back frae Afghanistan, fae Germany.
Thi licht wad faa oan onywan.

Ut pleys wi ma herr, burns ma nape,
ut passis thru ma banes an laives spores
therr o daurkniss ayont aa dawins.

Thi cat dwaums o parlaments
o heidliss mice. Eh'm lukein thru'ur
intil thon nicht ayont bombs, ayont money,

whaur fowk stoap oan brigs owre thi Clyde,
thi Neva, an waatch thi licht arrive
fae extink stars, an wait fur thi licht

fae thi stars yet tae come.

II To Yeltsin (1992)

I am dead, but you
are living
Boris Pasternak
Doctor Zhivago

As thi furst bids arrehv fur Lenin's banes
twa blimps ascend abune Red Square:
yin says *Pola*, thi ithir *Cola*. Ilkane

---

sark-vest; *wame*-belly, womb; *poke*-pouch; *unca*-unusually;
ayont-beyond; *dwaums*-dreams; *abune*-above.

282

costs saxty thoosan dollars. Thi date
is May thi Furst, but nae tanks gee thanks
tae you, as ye maun've calculatit

lang syne. Thi furst buds push thru
this English gairdin lyk fingirtips:
Eh wundir gin Eh tuke thir prints

wad Eh get sodgers, husbands, Man-
delstam? An yet ye hud tae repress
thon camsteery core o celebrants

o Stalin's burthday — sae Freudian
an act ut wad be tactless tae add
thi Capitalist's platitude

concernin thi Unearnin's gratitude
gin ye didnae sae brawly deserve ut
fur duntin yir last heid-bummir oot,

wha wadna hasten Russia's race
tae buy hur freedom frae thi West
when serfitude wiz aa yi could

invest. Eh waatch thi dentylions
brent thru thi southren simmer green
lyk black mairt brollies, bairgain boambs,

or jist thi plooks oan thi Urse's hide
as seen frae space by Krikalev,
thon cosmonaut that sat ootside

aa cheenge, angelickly-aware
thru radio hams o coup an you,
o Commonwealth an thon's despair,

---

camsteery-fierce, perverse; *heid-bummir*-leader; *dentylions*-
dandylions; *brent*-burst, leap; *mairt*-market; *urse*-bear.

thi last tae ride thi yirthly crest,
thi furst tae cross owre concepts; no
thi achronic birl o dogma's collar.

Eh think o Scoatlan, still stapt ticht
in uts disunity, lyk Auld Nick's
three-heidit doag in wan slip leash;

and Dante wiz sae subtly richt
tae tell himsel tae nivir retour,
no jist tae Florence, his past hame,

but tae thi past in Florentine heids,
thir indecisive noo. Dundee
wad be lyk landin fae thon heicht,

breathan thi Steppes' uncheengin air.

III To Rutskoi (1993)
Our concern is humon wholeness — the child-like spirit
Newborn every day —
Hugh MacDarmid
Third Hymn to Lenin

As Eh exhaled, trehin tae relax,
Eh heard thi saulter i thi field ootside
whinny, and Eh thocht o thon

puir cuddie in Kutznetsky Street
that Mayakovsky waatcht faa doon,
be whuppit as ut pechd uts life awa.

---

stapt-rammed; *retour*-return; *trehin*-trying; *saulter*-horse that
jumps in events; *cuddie*-horse;
peched-panted.

284

That wiz whit yi ettlet tae dae
tae thon sair forfochen nag
caad 'Communism' thi ither dey.

Did you no ken tho histry micht
repeat, lyk a wean that huztae eat
naethin but the rehet kail o

slaistery theory, ut nivir can
repeal utsel? Eh luke oot meh windie at
thae horsis that, like me, nivir hud

tae pu as muckle's Orwell's Boxer,
an think we hae medd fictions here
o yir followers' rarest hopes;

fur whit wiz Timex but a tale telt
tae richtless warkirs by thir
virrless union, tae keep thum aa

fae kennan o thir knackirt faa
intae fause timelessness, thi pasture
o a militatin posture.

Aa you did wiz add some killin,
tae mak ut mair Leniny, tae gee ye mair
1917-esque a feelin.

An sae thi tincan cavalry came at last
but no tae sain ye by thi pooer
o thi haimmer an Rab Sorbie,

---

ettlet-attempted; *sair forfochen*-very bewildered, exhausted;
rehet-reheated; *slaistery*-slimy; *as muckle's*-as much as; *virrless*-
impotent; *fause*-false; *sain*-protect from harm by a ritual sign;
Rab Sorbie-sickle.

but, fur twa an a plack o promises
fae Yeltsin, tae mak thi nicht
a dingle-dousie o tracer fire,

a swack an dinnil o rinny daith
in oaffices and oan stairwells. Still
Eh'm vanein at thon gripy bairn,

ridan oan thi back o a bear,
bringan thi Apocalypse o statelessness,
thi furst lowsan-time

o thi reins an bridle o thi harns.

---

twa and a plack-a considerable amount; *dingle-dousie*-a lighted
stick waved rapidly in the dark to form an arc of light; *swack*-a
sudden heavy blow; *dinnil*-vibration; *vanein*-calling a horse in
harness to turn to the left; *lowsan-time*-the time for unyoking
horses; *harns*-brains.

Stateless

Linda France

Tavarisch is a dirty word. Blue-pencilled
like an official secret. The built-in obsolescence
of perestroika, Leningrad, Space Station Mir.
My mother was so proud. Now Cosmonaut Krikalev
is just a repairman, Robinson Crusoe in overalls,
a hero for a country that doesn't exist.

When I was afraid of the dark, my mother
told me I could switch it on, like light.
And she'd show me the stars, families
of silver bears. Now I can't switch it off.
So many different shades of black,
clouds of stars and sewage. The only
lovely thing is earth, tantalising,
forbidden as a black-market apple.

First, the floating frogs kept us busy,
research. Then the quail chicks started
dying and everything went wrong like a joke
won't survive re-telling. I'm still
waiting for the punch-line: choke
on the glutinous food, reconstituted air.
Nothing like home. My family on TV
at the weekends: coloured postcards
I can't keep. I switch off the machine,
stare at its dark. Get back to my exercises.

I don't know if there'll be a party
when I come home: dancing, scarlet
in the streets, my name in the stars, medals
forged from melted missiles. Anything
would be better than what I don't know
already, everything I know about dark.

287

May Day

Dinah Livingstone

A May morning at Minsmere,
in the bird reserve, many calls
I can't identify — some singing,
some sound more conversational
and the bass is the rhythm of the sea.

Before me in young leaf the May tree
stands frothing with starry blossom,
milky sunlit epiphany:
in admiration hope does not fail.

The tree is thick and squat,
its comfortable shape,
tousled on top,
spikes the hazy blue
now clearing to speedwell.

Its flowering month
opens with that annual outburst
of belief in life before death,
faith leading to insight
of a species as whole-heartedly human
as it is most tranquilly tree.

Of course they want to cancel it.
These bosses despise
workers, makers, seers,
deny their holiday.
Time runs out on earth.
May Day. May Day. May Day...

History Never Happened

Mr Social Control

Work
Was born
In a deep and dirty ditch,
In the days of ancient Babylon in nights as black as pitch,
The very first prisoners from the first war were trapped,
And set to digging irrigation for some gits in ziggurats,
And when the overseers saw how the work got done,
They got the whole population down to join in the fun,
Since then things have gone downhill, we're neck-deep in
    the stench,
History never happened, we're still digging the same trench,
This organised misanthropy puts hatred in my heart,
So I get revenged upon the world by simply taking part,
History, it never happened.

And in the crooked march of centuries the 20th's a blip,
A century of dreams from welfare state to rocketship,
Nye Bevan and Apollo in irrelevant modernity
Fell away to leave us face to face with all eternity,
So the next one is the last one, the pseudo-Victorian fallacy
Began as fancy lamp-posts, ended up as public policy,
So beggars on Gin Alley are cluttering the kerbs,
The Navy is delivering ultimata to the Serbs,
There was no Great Leap Forward and no Treaty of Wien,
You make me feel like it's almost 1815 again.

One time we said we will be poor no more John Maynard
     Keynes,
And he said, cool, I'll pay you well to make washing
     machines,
And parts of carburettors and a splendid safety net,
To spend your brand-new wages on and make you all forget
That one time you had threatened us, the terms of this
     petition
Were historically specific as there's no human condition,
Too flexible, too durable, so day by day we manage,
Committing grace and patience and the odd criminal
     damage.

And when we get on to the salaries of those chaps who run
     British Gas,
We get this rhetorical pronoun makes us sound like we
     think we're a class,
And when I signed on they were tricking me, into feeling
     like I was thieving,
And I really am totally pig-sick of ducking and diving and
     dodging and weaving.
Holocaust? Which Holocaust? I made it all up in my
     bedroom,
History's just a mass break-out of the famous False
     Memory Syndrome.

And even then back in Babylon, museums housed the past,
They thought they were the crown of ages come to fruit at
     last,
A history of gangstas since, writ just to misinform,
Writing itself was devised by bureaucrats using cuneiform,
To proclaim the End of History, stagflation, boom and bust,
All built on the illusion that it ever will be thus,
Which it will if it's allowed to, for there's just one chance I
     get,
That history never happened, as it hasn't started yet.

We enter by the tavern door, we laugh and buy our round,
And really it don't matter, soon enough we're in the ground,
And everything we do, say, love, smell, overthrow or taste,
Was just one single moment in annihilation's waste,
And when the last ten bricks of London are consumed into
    the clay,
When the last of tombs has perished and there's two nights
    every day,
When the Sun's gone supergiant there will be no breath to
    say
That history never happened because we let it slip away.

The evolution of chaotic systems
Is characterised by sudden cataclysms,
Highly determined, unexpected transitions
From one semi-stable state to the next,
The flap of that proverbial butterfly's wing
Looses the lightning above Beijing,
You change the world when you change one thing,
Like in that film.

And we're ready for the kick-off,
Like the First World War,
We're ready for the kick-off,
And all we need's a bullet through a fat arch-duke.

The Shoes of Dead Comrades

Jackie Kay

On my father's feet are the shoes of dead comrades.
Gifts from the comrades' sad red widows.
My father would never see good shoes go to waste.
Good brown leather, black leather, leather soles.
Doesn't matter if they are a size too big, small.

On my father's feet are the shoes of dead comrades.
The marches they marched against Polaris. UCS.
Everything they ever believed tied up with laces.
A cobbler has replaced the sole, the heel.
Brand new, my father says, look, feel.

On my father's feet are the shoes of dead comrades.
These are in good nick. These were pricey.
Italian leather. See that. Lovely.
He always was a classy dresser was Arthur.
Ever see Wullie dance? Wullie was a wonderful waltzer.

On my father's feet are the shoes of dead comrades.
It scares me half to death to consider
that one day it won't be Wullie or Jimmy or Arthur,
that one day someone will wear the shoes of my father,
the brown and black leather of all the dead comrades.

News From Nowhere

John Lucas

That rotting breath was cider
drunk to ease a cancered throat
though pain sharpened his eyes
to vistas lost from trudged streets

where still he fattened dreams for Xmas cheer:
"String the bloody tories from lamp-posts
with gold balls rammed in their mouths."
A year later that voice

like kerb-roughened steel came growling
"another poxy day in this blighted place,"
then, turning against my shrug —
"the right weather for no-hopers."

One morning he was missing. "Next
Door was forced to break in.
Well, he'd nothing much to live for,"
was all our new, young postman said.

That night I dreamed of messages
brought from some beleaguered state
whose wind-torn shutters rasped
of broken cities needing to be re-built,

and through next morning's wet
of news was listening still
for his incurable sound
his wakening words.

Ringstead Mill

Margot Heinemann

Stranger whom I once knew well,
Do not haunt this house.
Sorrow's but a ravelled thread
To draw back the active dead,
Nor is pleasure mutable
Such as smiled on us.
Stranger whom I once knew well,
Do not haunt this house.

Idle and low spirits can
Take your name and face:
Old green sweater, battered coat,
Coal-black hair and sleeves too short —
Though I know the living man
Finished with this place,
Idle and low spirits can
Take your name and face.

Here we laid foundations where
Never walls were built.
Faded is the fireside glow,
Things we knew or seemed to know
Blown across the trackless air,
And the milk is spilt.
Here we laid foundations where
Never walls were built.

And the hard thing to believe
Still is what you said.
With a bullet in the brain,
How can matter think again?
All things that once live and move
Endlessly are dead.
And the hard thing to believe
Still is what you said.

So from these deserted rooms
Even memory's past.
As your closely-pencilled screed
Grows more faint and hard to read,
So our blueprints and our dreams,
Torn from time, are lost,
And from these deserted rooms
Even memory's passed.

Mountains that we saw far off,
Sleek with gentle snow,
To the climber's axe reveal
Ice that jars the swinging steel,
Armoured on a holdless cliff
With the clouds below —
Mountains that we saw far off,
Sleek with gentle snow.

Time bears down its heroes all
And the fronts they held.
Yet their charge of change survives
In the changed fight of our lives —
Poisoned fires they never dreamed of
Ring the unrented field.
Change is their memorial
Who have changed the world.

Note:
Ringstead Mill was found among Margot Heinemann's papers
after her death and was written in 1990 or 1991. The poem was
read at her funeral by Tilda Swinton. Ringstead Mill was
handwritten and it was not clear whether the word in the third
last line was *unrented* or *untented*.

Produce of Cyprus

Alison Brackenbury

Picking grapes from a paper bag, sucking the misted skin
I think of the island which grew them, Venus' ground
(the rain is in sheets on my window, wet, green, blind)
there, the dry song of the cicada, there the warm nights
with the window propped open, sea's stripe on the
    counterpane.

Yet they too, have their troubles. The frosts were late;
the land does not love us, relentless stony ground,
though we own it down generations. The price of grapes
is falling; and so on. No doubt they dream of us
that far and prosperous country; on its window, the
    wealth of the rain.

The last is tough. The bag, as I put by the rest
rustles and whispers, Paradise is the place
of which we know nothing, which we know best.

Rain Falls on Utopia Too

Arnold Rattenbury

Whispers run and trip down the pebbled
track where harebells bob, And then
a field of nesty late-crop grass,
soon to be hay, snatches the rumour,
flurries round banner-weeds, and the track
clatters into procession.
                    Run,
Defend yourself, No time, They're coming,
Are here.
       But rain is not a threat,
you panickers in the wind — fieldmice,
muttering pebbles, gossip grass,
harebells that duck expected blows
on the back. A likely change of weather,
nothing to fear, a benison,
a thing allowed for.
              Sir, it will swamp
our nests and make this track a river
pouring straight to your door, beat
us about the heads. Sir, it will flatten
the hay, disprofit men.
            Why, so
it may. That is the way of change
you taught from the start, from not-so-high
to the tall grass, a-crawl on pebbles,
eye-to-eye with wildflowers. That
is the dangerous way of all the change
we dream, then wake to pre-arrange.

                * * *

Some there must be who make do
in a city, or write at all in a city.
Words must correspond to a sense
of something there. It takes all kinds
to make a literature.
                    This gardening
kind, for one — in this ungardened
fieldscape: what's to be done, and Nature
to do it with, both evident.

And so he digs for sense (as the saying
is), pulls words for weeds and shores
up things mistakenly disturbed:
rain, that he hopes delayed till digging
is done, will settle them. Language
has roots as well.
                    Hearing the starts
and sibilance all Nature hears,
he scuttles in like a mouse. Inside
the house, darkness is of the sudden
sort that speaks of weaknesses.

All Nature concerns him. He
is a kind of man. Mankind's in pain.
Meaning's a kind of hide-and-seek
he digs for. Mostly — men are in cities
far from here, this place and act
where practically no men are.

* * *

Countries glitter with promise at each
return; and rain, in this event
enhances that — beaten bell-heads
are jewelled, and all the defeated blades
in silver splinters. True, the hay
lies ruined, a river pours to the door,
nests are awash. And sure, a messed-
up dig affects his plan.
                                    What
reasons suggests that it should not?
Only folly would let suppose
some neater things than what he knows
must be — for all well-reasoned process.
Nature proceeds, by revolution,
season to season, class from class;
is beat sometimes — by drought, pollution,
plagues of insects, floods, crews
of piratical goats (for this is Wales),
rabbits.
            There sir, frighten yourself.
Wars cross fences. Murder screams
down the air to dig up more than gardens.
After you win, if you do, revanche
attacks.
            Ah, but there's Paradise
pre-arranged — even, though how heaven knows,
in cities. In the washed air, it glows.

Acknowledgements

Copyright is held by the individual authors or their estates unless otherwise stated, and poems are reprinted by permission. Please contact Five Leaves if you wish to be put in touch with copyright holders. The cover illustration is by Clifford Harper.

Valentine Ackland's *Communist Poem, 1935* was first published in *Left Review*, June 1935, © Carcanet Press and reprinted by permission of Susanna Pinney; *About Benwell* by Gillian Allnutt is from *Blackthorn* (Bloodaxe Books, 1994); *Cuba, Crocodiles, Rain* by Keith Armstrong was first published in *Pains of Class* (Artery Publications, London, 1982); *Adam* by Honor Arundel appeared in *New Lyrical Ballads* edited by Honor Arundel, Maurice Carpenter and Jack Lindsay (Poetry London Editions, 1945) and is © Jessica Balfour and Catherine Kerr-Dineen; Neil Astley's *East of Easter* is from *Biting My Tongue* (Bloodaxe Books, 1995); *Musée des Beaux Arts* was published in *Another Time* (Faber, 1940) © the Estate of WH Auden; George Barker's *O Hero Akimbo on the Mountains of Tomorrow* was first published in *Poems for Spain* (ed) John Lehmann and Stephen Spender (Hogarth Press, 1939), © Elspeth Barker; *David Guest* by Martin Bell appeared in his *Collected Poems 1937-66* (Macmillan, 1967); *The Gaudy Camp Follower* by Jack Beeching is from *Poems 1940-*2000 (Collection Myrtus, 2001) by Jack Beeching, section 7, *Climbers, Riders, Lovers*; *My Song is for All Men* by Peter Blackman was first published by Lawrence and Wishart, 1952; *Confessions of an Old Believer* is the title poem of Jim Burns' collection published by Redbeck Press (Bradford, 1996); Alison Brackenbury's *Produce of Cyprus* is from her *Selected Poems* (Carcanet, 1991, © Alison Brackenbury, 1988); *Baz and the Freedom of the Press* by Kevin Cadwallender appears in *Public* (Iron Press); *The Fallen Elm* by John Clare is reproduced by permission of Curtis Brown Group Ltd on behalf of Eric Robinson, © Eric Robinson; *Notes for My Son* by Alex Comfort © Nicholas Comfort; *Full Moon at Tierz* (from *Left* Review, March 1937) and *Poem* (from *New Writing*, Autumn 1937) by John Cornford appears by permission of James Cornford; Joe Corrie's poems are reprinted by permission of Morag Corrie, *The Image o' God* is from *The Image o' God* (Porpoise Press, 1937) and *Rebel Tam* is from *Joe Corrie: plays, poems and theatre writings* (7.84 Publications, 1985).

The Beasts of England was first published in Andy Croft's *Just as Blue* (Flambard, 2001); *To Eat To-day* by Nancy Cunard appears by permission of A.R.A. Hobson as representative of the Heirs of Nancy Cunard and was first published in the *New Statesman* on 1st October, 1938; Julia Darling's *Poverty* appeared in *Small Beauties* (Newcastle City Libraries); C. Day Lewis' poems were first published in *The Magnetic Mountain* (Hogarth, 1933) © the Day Lewis estate and the Peters Fraser Dunlop Group; *Children of Wealth* by Elizabeth Daryush © Carcanet Press; Idris Davies' poems are reprinted by permission of Ceinfryn and Gwyn Morris, *The Angry Summer* was first published by Faber, 1943,

Adrian Mitchell is an internationally-acclaimed poet, playwright and novelist who has given more than 1,000 poetry performances all over the world. His books of poems include *Heart on the Left: Poems 1953-84*, *Blue Coffee*, *All Shook Up* and *Balloon Lagoon*. Among his plays are *Tyger Two*, *Satie Day/Night* and *Man Friday*, as well as many distinguished adaptations for the British theatre, including *Marat/Sade*, *The Mayor of Zalamea*, *Peer Gynt*, *Fuente Ovejuna* and *The Government Inspector*. His plays for children include three plays with songs based on the Beatrix Potter stories and *The Lion, the Witch and the Wardrobe*. He is married, has five children, seven grandchildren and describes himself as a socialist-anarchist pacifist. He was recently appointed Shadow Poet Laureate by *Red Pepper* magazine.

Andy Croft lives in Middlesbrough, where he has been active for many years in community writing projects. He has published widely on the literary history of the British Labour Movement, including *Red Letter Days*, *Out of the Old Earth*, *A Weapon in the Struggle*, *Selected Poems of Randall Swingler* and *Comrade Heart*.

He has written thirty-two books for teenagers, mostly about football, and published five books of poetry — *Nowhere Special*, *Gaps Between Hills*, *Headland*, *Just as Blue* and *Great North*. He is currently Writer-in-Residence at HMP Holme House, Stockton. He was a member of the Communist Party until its demise in 1991.